D1358502

COPYRIGHT ©1998
CENTER FOR FAMILY LIFE, INC.

PUBLISHED BY:

CENTER FOR FAMILY LIFE, INC.
3611 Farquhar Avenue - Suite 3
Los Alamitos, CA 90720

$11.95 Soft Cover
Printed in the United States of America

I S B N Number: 0-9623986-2-4

Portions of pages 50 through 54, 57 through 64 are reproduced from *How to Live With Your Teenager, Vol. I - A Survivor's Handbook for Parents* by Peter H. Buntman, M.S.W., ACSW and Eleanor Saris M.Ed.

(First Printing 1998)

FORWARD

The specific methods we teach in this book on how to get your ADHD children to behave and to do better in school were developed over twenty years of working with ADHD children and their families at the Center For Family Life, Inc. Parents were able to use our methods immediately after reading this material and they were able to help their children to behave in school and at home.

When we gave review copies to parents prior to publication, many of them wanted space to take notes. We deliberately created this publication with a blank page side-by-side with each page for your notes and reminders.

Peter H. Buntman, M.S.W., ACSW, Licensed Clinical Social Worker

DEDICATION

To Karla, my wife, whom I remain as eternally smitten as the first day. To my children; Scotty, age 4 and Riley, age 8, who teach me about nurturing and giving everyday.

ACKNOWLEDGMENT

My very special thanks to Pat Tanaka who worked endlessly typing the manuscript for this book and the revisions and revisions and revisions.

DEALING WITH MOM'S ANGER

Portions of pages 45 through 47 of this Information Guide

are reproduced from pages 97 through 102 of the book

HOW TO LIVE WITH YOUR TEENAGER: A SURVIVOR'S HANDBOOK FOR PARENTS

by, Peter H. Buntman, M.S.W., ACSW and Eleanor M. Saris, M.Ed.

TABLE OF CONTENTS

CHAPTER ONE: How Does It Feel To Be A Mom Of An ADHD Child?
Pages 6 through 9

CHAPTER TWO: What Is It Like To Be An ADHD Child?
Pages 10 through 13

CHAPTER THREE: What Do We Know About ADHD?
Page 14

CHAPTER FOUR: The Signs And Symptoms Of ADHD
Pages 15 through 16

CHAPTER FIVE: All That's Hyperactive Isn't Hyperactivity
Pages 17 through 25

        SECTION A: Early Childhood Trauma - Page 19

        SECTION B: Learning Disability - Page 20 through 21

        SECTION C: Organicity - Page 22

        SECTION D: Epilepsy and Seizure Disorder - Page 23

        SECTION E: Lead Poisoning - Page 24 through 25

CHAPTER SIX: How To Get Your Child To Behave And Listen To You, Part I
Pages 26 through 41

CHAPTER SEVEN: How To Get Your Child To Behave And Listen To You, Part II
Pages 42 through 44

CHAPTER EIGHT: Dealing With Mom's Anger
Pages 45 through 47

CHAPTER NINE: How To Get Your Child To Go To Sleep
Pages 48 through 49

CHAPTER TEN: Self-Esteem
Pages 50 through 56

CHAPTER ELEVEN: School Problems
Pages 57 through 59

CHAPTER TWELVE: The ADHD Child And The School System
Pages 60 through 67

CHAPTER THIRTEEN: Medications
Pages 68 through 71

CHAPTER FOURTEEN: Questions From Parents
Pages 72 through 79

CHAPTER ONE: **How Does It Feel to Be The Mom Of An ADHD Child?**

This story is typical of the moms we see in our office, who come in to get help for their children with ADHD:

Barbara walked into the office, sat down on the couch, and began to cry. "I'm gonna kill him!" she sobbed.

I asked her, "Why do you want to kill him?"

Mom replied, " I feel like a total failure! I teach second grade, and I win awards all the time for being a great teacher, and my four-and-a-half-year-old son has been thrown out of his third preschool!"

When I asked him why he got thrown out of his third preschool, she proceeded to tell me, "He bit another child in the class!"

I then asked mom, "What led up to this?"

Mom explained through her tears, "He can't stay in line! Whenever there are lines for recess, the water fountain, the bathroom, or anything, he pushes to the head of the line. He hits the other children. He shoves them and if they hit him back he has a temper tantrum or shoves them back and bites them. When he bit a child two days ago, he actually drew blood!" That's when the preschool expelled him."

I questioned mom further by asking, "What other behaviors does he display at school?"

Mom replied, "He fidgets. He moves around and he can't sit still for more than two or three minutes. He wanders around the classroom. He calls out to the teacher and interrupts her for no reason. He wasn't expelled from the preschool for walking around the room. The reason he was expelled from the preschool was for hitting and biting other children."

"Tell me what else is going on with your son." I said. "What's his behavior like at home?"

Mom exclaimed, "He's a nightmare! He's always picking and hitting at his two-and-a-half-year- old brother. A week ago I caught him on top of his two-and-a-half-year-old brother who was turning blue. He was choking him and I think he would have killed him if I hadn't pulled him off!"

Mom continued, "His behavior drives me nuts at home! He won't sit still. He won't listen to me! He's like a little whirlwind of motion who is running around and doing anything he wants!"

I then asked mom, "What's dinner like?"

Mom told me, "He'll throw milk at his brother, food on the floor and won't sit still!"

When I asked her what time her son went to sleep she replied, "He's up at a quarter to six. He will not take a nap at school. He will not take a nap at home. He finally goes to bed sometime between quarter of twelve and twelve midnight!"

I asked her, "What do you do to discipline him?"

Mom said, "It doesn't matter. Whatever I do doesn't work. I've tried giving him time-outs. I've tried spanking him. I've tried taking away his toys and Nintendo. I've tried taking away the TV. I've even tried a combination of all of these; but whatever I try, it doesn't work!"

I then inquired, "What types of discipline does he receive at school?"

"They give him time-outs or they put him in a corner. Whatever disciplines he gets at school or at home; they don't help."

When I asked her if her husband helped, she told me, "He doesn't! He says he won't eat with the children because he gets pains in his stomach."

Mom continued, "My husband goes to work really early and he stays really late. He tells me that he's avoiding the children because he doesn't like to be around them. He says they won't listen to him. He gets angry and then he starts yelling and shouting and calling names and swearing. This isn't good!"

I asked what was going on during the weekends at home and mom said, "Well, I have them all day. My husband goes to work although he doesn't have to. He owns his own business; but he wants to avoid the children. It's easier for him to be at work than to be at home."

My next question to mom was, "How do you and your husband get along?" I then asked, "How often do you and your husband get out at night?"

Mom answered, "We never go out. We never get any breaks. Every thirteen-, fourteen- or fifteen-year-old neighborhood girl knows us. A babysitter only lasts one night. We can't get anyone to babysit a second time because the children are so terrible!"

I asked, "How are you and your husband doing?"

She answered, "We're not! We are exhausted all the time. We fight and argue a lot. There's never any time just for ourselves. We never talk about anything except the children and how they are driving us nuts. We still care about each other; but we're so exhausted taking care of these children, we have no time for ourselves."

"Tell me how you are feeling" I said.

Mom replied, "There are some days that I don't even get up in the morning. I get really down and depressed. I have feelings like I wish I never had these children! I have feelings like I wish these children were never born! I wish I could give them away! I wish I could go away for six months, start a new life and not come back!"

Barbara is typical of many of the moms we see at our office. I always say, half jokingly, that I can always tell if there's an ADHD child by looking at the mom; by how exhausted she is. ADHD moms feel exhausted, depressed, angry and frustrated. Typically, as with Barbara, the marriage isn't doing well because both partners are so exhausted from taking care of their child that they don't have any time to themselves. They don't go out because they can't get babysitters. They don't communicate well or have quality "alone" time because all of their time and energies go into caring for the children. In addition, they are so exhausted that they don't have a sex life.

Barbara's feelings are typical of ADHD moms. These moms often feel like they wish they had never had the child. They feel like they wish the child had never been born. They feel like they wish the child would run away. They wish they could run away. They feel depressed. One mom told me, "I feel like a victim who is being punished all of the time. I'm out of energy. It's like having a car that's out of gas. When a car doesn't have gas, it can't run. I've been running on empty for years!"

Unlike moms with children who don't have an ADHD problem, (those who can get babysitters, who can go to bed at a reasonable hour, who can get a break when their children take naps) these moms with ADHD children often never get any rest. This goes on from fourteen to eighteen hours a day seven days a week.

Among the many things that frustrate moms, one is that no matter what they do, it doesn't help their child. Whatever type of discipline or punishment they give; it doesn't help. They try time-outs; it doesn't help. They spank; it doesn't help. They take privileges away such as the TV, the Nintendo, a favorite toy, a favorite animal; but it doesn't help. With older children, they make them write sentences; it doesn't help. When they try a combination of punishments, it doesn't help.

One mother told me, " I have two children and it takes twenty times more energy to parent my ADHD child than my other child. I have to put twenty times more effort, energy and time into it. It's not fair!"

Moms typically feel it's unfair. They ask, "Why does this happen to me?"

Moms feel hopeless. They feel that things will never change. This, for many moms, increases their frustration, anger and depression.

Approximately 75% of the ADHD moms say their husbands don't help very much. To generalize in our society, moms tend to be much better parents than dads. Dads usually don't have the coping skills necessary to deal with ADHD children. They get frustrated, call names and get angry. Dads simply don't know what to do with their ADHD child.

CHAPTER TWO: What Is It Like To Be An ADHD Child?

Because of his behavior, the ADHD child often feels like he's cursed and a failure. Also because of his behavior, he's constantly getting into trouble at school and at home. All of the attention brought to him is negative.

It's not, "Good going, Johnny!" It's, "Johnny, you goofed up again!"

Whenever he's happy and experiences joy, the ADHD child instantly is struck down with, "You goofed up again!"

It doesn't take very long for the ADHD child to feel terrible inside. That he's no good, worthless, valueless and that there's something "wrong" with him.

The ADHD child also feels "dumb" and "stupid" because he can't get along in school, has trouble learning and concentrating.

Because of the nature of ADHD, the child has a hard time making friends. He can't play cooperatively because of impulsivity. He often pushes, shoves and kicks the other children which makes the other children avoid him and not play with him.

Many activities such as Little League, AYSO soccer, Boy Scouts, Girl Scouts, Brownies, Cub Scouts and Church Youth Groups involve sharing. They require cooperative play time. However, the ADHD child has a real problem sharing because of his lack of impulse control.

*****

Let's take the following typical day in the life of an ADHD child:

You're six and a half years old and your name is Bill. When you get up in the morning your mom tells you to brush your teeth and get dressed. After you get dressed you go downstairs for breakfast. You heard mom say, "Brush your teeth," but you didn't remember it. When mom asks, "Did you brush your teeth?" you look at her blankly because you don't know how to say you didn't know she told you. Mom says, "You didn't! How many times do I have to tell you to do something? Don't you understand the English language?" You feel you have messed up and mom doesn't feel any caring and warmth for you and is angry with you.

You go back upstairs, brush your teeth and come back downstairs to find breakfast on the table. Mom and dad are eating with your nine-year-old brother. You've got scrambled eggs and toast waiting for you. Dad is talking to mom about something you're not very interested

in so you take the fork and eat your eggs. You're not hungry so you start playing with the fork. Tapping it and moving the eggs off of the plate. Suddenly, a whole bunch of eggs falls off of the plate and onto the floor. Dad smacks you on the arm and shouts, "Can't you ever pay attention to what you're doing you stupid jerk!?"

You feel really bad inside. You want dad to be happy with you but he just yelled at you again and your arm hurts where he smacked you. You remember that dad has told you that before but you just got involved with the eggs and forgot completely.

You finish breakfast and mom tells you, "Go upstairs, get your jacket and put it on, and I'll walk you to the school bus." You go upstairs and you turn the Nintendo on because you want to play with it. Mom comes upstairs three or four minutes later and screams at you, "Why did you turn on the Nintendo? You're going to be late for the bus!" Mom grabs you by the arm, throws your jacket at you and pushes you to go downstairs. You know mom is angry with you again.

On the bus you sit down next to Ralph, a boy you want to have as a friend. He gets up and says, "I don't want to sit near you! You're a jerk!" Then all of the other kids laugh and say, "Yeah! You're the guy who starts fights and trouble all of the time!" They all move away from you and you feel something's wrong with you. You wonder why no one wants to be your friend.

You get to school and the teacher begins the day with a coloring project in which everyone has to draw a picture with crayons. She explains the project and you don't want to do it so you shout out at the teacher, "When are we gonna have recess?"

All of the other children laugh and the teacher angrily says, "How many times do I have to tell you?! Don't interrupt me and don't speak without raising your hand!" You remember she has said that many times but you forgot because you didn't want to do the coloring; you wanted to go out to recess.

The coloring isn't very interesting to you, so when you heard a bird at the window, you decided to go out and walk there. The teacher said to you, "Why are you wandering around the room? Go back and do your coloring!" You can't understand why she's so upset because the coloring isn't any fun anyway.

The class finally goes out to recess. The boys are playing a game with a ball in which they kick it back and forth to each other. They're not kicking it to you and you run over and grab the ball from another boy. He pushes you and you push him back and the two of you get into

a fist fight. The teacher comes over to the fight and screams, "I can't leave you alone for two minutes! You always pick on other people and get into fights!"

During the course of the school day, Bill is reprimanded as many as five to ten times. He then goes home to mom.

Although almost all ADHD children are extremely bright and have average to above average intelligence, by the nature of their problem they are constantly disciplined by parents and teachers and receive negative feedback from their peers and friends. This makes them feel "dumb" and "stupid."

Going back to your scenario as Bill:

After school the bus took you home and mom took you to soccer practice. When you walked up to the bench two or three of the other children said, "Oh, there's Bill again! Coach, do we have to have him on our team?" You felt terrible.

The coach began explaining techniques on how to kick and pass the ball. You didn't understand it so you decided to walk off by yourself. The coach shouts, "Bill, come back here! How many times do I have to tell you to pay attention and not wander off!?"

Another child said, "Coach, can't we get rid of him? We hate him!" Again, you feel terrible.

When soccer practice was over the children began walking over to the area in which the moms parked their cars. Just then, one of the other boys turned around and said to you, "Don't ever come back here! We hate you! You're not a good player!"

You became angry and started a fist fight by jumping on the boy.

The moms and coach ran over to you and yelled, "Bill! You can't hit other people! Why do you keep doing that?!"

Your mom took you home and you were in a really bad mood because of the many people who had been on your case all day. Mom said to you, "Go clean up. We're going to eat in a half hour." You went upstairs and when you saw your four-and-a-half-year-old brother you pushed him and began to fight. You were taking your anger out on your brother.

*****

Life for an ADHD child is typically a world in which he is constantly being told he's "no good," he's "doing bad," he's "made mistakes," and he "won't listen," by parents, teachers at school, coaches and other adults.

Constantly, an ADHD child is being told he is wrong, stupid and dumb. He's told he doesn't listen, doesn't obey and he doesn't understand.

Each time a child is told these things, it makes him feel bad, terrible, stupid, dumb and that there is something wrong with him.

For the ADHD child, this is the story of his life day after day. Because of the nature of his problem, he gets disapproval, rejection, anger, scorn, hostility and negativity from parents, teachers, coaches, peers, friends, and virtually everyone in his world.

This goes on day after day, week after week, month after month, year after year.

How an ADHD child perceives the world is ground into him in the form of those messages that there is something wrong with him, he's no good, people are always angry at him, people don't like him, he's supposed to feel bad inside, and he's a failure.

CHAPTER THREE: **What Do We Know About Attention-Deficit/ Hyperactivity Disorders?**

We know that Attention-Deficit/Hyperactivity Disorder is a genetic problem that is inherited just like eye color and hair color or any other genetic characteristic. When we ask a mom a lot of questions about their family background, we can almost always find members of one of the parents' families that had these types of behaviors when they were a child.

We also know that ADHD occurs in boys much more often than in girls. Some research says four times as many boys have ADHD. Some says it's nine times as many boys than girls have ADHD.

When we get technical and make a diagnosis, we have Attention-Deficit/Hyperactivity Disorder combined type. Then we have Attention-Deficit Disorder/Hyperactivity Disorder predominantly inattention type. We also have Attention-Deficit Disorder/Hyperactivity Disorder predominantly hyperactive impulsive type.

Attention-Deficit Disorder is a problem with concentration. Hyperactivity is a problem of impulse control and excessive motor activity.

Children with Attention-Deficit/Hyperactivity Disorder predominantly inattention type don't cause their parents as many problems as the other two types.

These children seem to have more problems at school than at home and very often they "can slip through the cracks." However, it appears that with this type there are almost as many girls as boys.

CHAPTER FOUR: **The Signs And Symptoms Of ADHD**

The following is a chart from pages 83, 84 and 85 of the "Diagnostic and Statistical Manual of Mental Disorders, Fourth Edition." The book is also known as "DSM-IV." The charts contain the diagnostic criteria for Attention-Deficit/Hyperactivity Disorder:

A.   Either (1) or (2):

    1)   six (or more) of the following symptoms of INATTENTION have persisted for at least 6 months to a degree that is maladaptive and inconsistent with developmental level:

    INATTENTION

        a)   often fails to give close attention to details or makes careless mistakes in schoolwork, work, or other activities.

        b)   often has difficulty sustaining attention in tasks or play activiites

        c)   often does not seem to listen when spoken to directly

        d)   often does not follow through on instructions and fails to finish schoolwork, chores, or duties in the workplace (not due to oppositional behavior or failure to understand instructions)

        e)   often has difficulty organizing tasks and activities

        f)   often avoids, dislikes, or is reluctant to engage in tasks that require sustained mental effort (such as schoolwork or homework)

        g)   often loses things necessary for tasks or activities (e.g. toys, school assignments, pencils, books, or tools)

        h)   is often easily distracted by extraneous stimuli

        I)   is often forgetful in daily activities

    2)   six (or more) of the following symptoms of HYPERACTIVITY-IMPULSIVITY have persisted for at least 6 months to a degree that is maladaptive and inconsistent with developmental level:

HYPERACTIVITY

    a)   often fidgets with hands or feet or squirms in seat

    b)   often leaves seat in classroom or in other situations in which remaining seated is expected

    c)   often runs about or climbs excessively in situations in which it is inappropriate (in adolescents or adults, may be limited to subjective feelings of restlessness)

    d)   often has difficulty playing or engaging in leisure activities quietly.

    e)   is often "on the go" or often acts as if "driven by a motor"

    f)   often talks excessively

    g)   often blurts out answers before questions have been completed

    h)   often has difficulty awaiting turn

    I)   often interrupts or intrudes on others (e.g., butts into conversations or games)

B.   Some hyperactive-impulsive or inattentive symptoms that caused impairment were present before age 7 years.

C.   Some impairment from the symptoms is present in two or more settings (e.g., at school [or work] and at home.)

D.   There must be clear evidence of clinically significant impairment in social, academic, or occupational functioning.

E.   The symptoms do not occur exclusively during the course of Pervasive Development Disorder, Schizophrenia, or other Psychotic Disorder and are not better accounted for by another mental disorder (e.g., Mood Disorder, Anxiety Disorder, Dissociative Disorder, or a Personality Disorder.)

CHAPTER FIVE: All That's Hyperactive Isn't Hyperactivity

Many parents come into our office wanting help for their ADHD child. After doing an extensive background history (which just means we talk to parents and ask them an awful lot of questions) and in many cases doing neuropsychological and psychological testing, we find out that the child does not have ADHD.

There are a number of different problems that can present identical and/or similar symptoms to ADHD. The first step is to make a complete diagnosis. If it is not ADHD, we treat the problem. The treatments for other problems are often different than the treatment for the ADHD child.

QUESTION: What other conditions can present symptoms similar to ADHD?

ANSWER: One is an Oppositional-Defiant Disorder.

QUESTION: What is an Oppositional-Defiant Disorder?

ANSWER: Children with an Oppositional-Defiant Disorder are usually strong-willed, stubborn, and want to get their way all of the time. They want what they want, when they want it.

These children tend to be very oppositional and defiant towards parents and teachers. One of the most striking features of an Oppositional-Defiant child is that they are self-destructive. When they violate parents' and teachers' rules, they get punished. This behavior deprives them of better relationships with parents and doing well in school and is extremely self-destructive.

When confronted with the fact that he has broken a rule, the Oppositional-Defiant Disorder child usually refuses to obey or he argues. If you ask him to stop something, he will go ahead and do it anyway.

These children can also be very antagonistic to their peers and are likely to have temper tantrums. Other characteristics of an Oppositional-Defiant Disorder Child are being negative and stubborn, they procrastinate and resist all rules of authority.

These children don't see their behavior as "wrong" but they see that the difficulties they are having are coming from their parents, friends and teachers who are making demands that aren't reasonable.

QUESTION: Can a child be ADHD and Oppositional-Defiant Disorder?

ANSWER: Yes. However, if the child has ODD only and not ADHD, we would treat him very differently in counseling.

SECTION A: Early Childhood Trauma

QUESTION: What else can a child have that would present symptoms similar to ADHD?

ANSWER: One is Early Childhood Trauma.

QUESTION: What is Early Childhood Trauma?

ANSWER: It's something that happened in the first few years of a child's life. Typically, up to age four or five, it's something in a child's past that created an emotional trauma.

QUESTION: What could some of these things be?

ANSWER: Some things that can cause this are: 1. Parents who are going through a difficult time in their marriage and argue in front of the children. 2. The parents separate or reconcile or divorce. 3. A child's grandparent can die and the child was very close to the grandparent, or the parent was close to the grandparent and went through a depression. 4. A parent can lose a job and be angry, upset or depressed. 5. A child can have a serious illness. 6. There can be a move to another house. 7. There can be a birth of a sibling. There are many other traumatic psychological events in a child's life.

QUESTION: Do all children who experience these types of things have "Childhood Trauma?"

ANSWER: No. But again, this early background needs to be looked at to see if this is the cause that is presenting the symptoms in a child that looks like ADHD.

Children with Early Childhood Trauma have Childhood Depression and Anxiety. Their behaviors and symptoms can look like ADHD.

SECTION B: Learning Disability

There are all sorts of different learning disabilities. Some of them have similar symptoms as ADHD. With Learning Disabilities, children exhibit problems in school.

Two of the major types of learning disabilities that we see are dyslexia and auditory processing problems.

QUESTION: What's dyslexia?

ANSWER: There are six different types of dyslexia. Usually it's a problem where children invert words or see them backwards and have a hard time reading. Their eyes get tired and they have a hard time concentrating. The symptoms can be similar to ADHD.

QUESTION: What's an auditory processing problem?

ANSWER: To be successful in school you need to be able to listen to and understand four different commands. For example; command number one to a third grade student is to take his Social Studies book out of the drawer. Command number two is to open the book to page 62. Command number three is to read the next twelve pages. Command number four is to write a two paragraph summary.

A child with an auditory processing problem can only hear and understand two commands. Because of a neurological or physiological impairment, he doesn't hear the last two commands.

Often the teacher can think a child is uncooperative, lazy, dumb, stupid and doesn't care.

QUESTION: How can I find out if my child has learning disabilities if I suspect he does?

ANSWER: We recommend that you take your child to a Neuropsychologist for psychological testing.

QUESTION: What is a Neuropsychologist?

ANSWER: A Neuropsychologist is a Psychologist who has specialized training in neurological mental health issues including ADHD and Learning Disabilities.

QUESTION: What happens when I take my child to a Neuropsychologist?

ANSWER: The Neuropsychologist will take background information and give the child a series of specialized tests. The Neuropsychologist will interpret, score and analyze the data then meet with the parents to give results of the testing.

QUESTION: What if the child has a Learning Disability, what happens then?

ANSWER: Depending on what the Learning Disability is, the Neuropsychologist can give you a plan to help the child with a Learning Disability.

SECTION C: **Organicity**

QUESTION: What is organicity?

ANSWER: With organicity a child's behavior or symptoms can be similar to ADD. It's caused by damage to a brain lobe.

QUESTION: How does damage to a brain lobe occur?

ANSWER: There are a number of ways this can occur. One way is through a difficult birth; it being a long extended birth or the use of forceps at birth. A more common way that damage to a brain lobe occurs is through some type of head injury. Every little baby falls down and hurts his head. Sometimes mother sees it and sometimes she doesn't. We always ask a mother, "Has your child ever hurt his head?" We always ask, "Has your child ever hit his head?" or "Did anyone hit him?" We ask, "Did he fall and hit his head?" Even if mothers don't see these falls, and often they don't, there still could be a head injury involved.

QUESTION: What does organicity actually mean?

ANSWER: It means there's physical damage to a brain lobe. We can do a lot in short-term counseling to change the behaviors that this causes.

QUESTION: How do you find this out?

ANSWER: We have a Neuropsychologist do testing. If any of these tests pick up suspicion of organicity that requires additional testing, we refer the child to a Neurologist. A Neurologist will administer specific tests such as an EEG, MRI or a BEAM.

QUESTION: What's a "BEAM"? I've never head of that.

ANSWER: One way to explain the BEAM is that, it's roughly like a 3-D color CAT scan of the brain. If there is organicity present, then the BEAM can help pinpoint the area.

SECTION D: **Epilepsy and Seizure Disorder**

Epilepsy and Seizure Disorders can also cause symptoms similar to ADD or Hyperactivity.

QUESTION: If a child has Epilepsy or Seizure Disorders, doesn't he have seizures or epileptic fits; grand mals or petite mals?

ANSWER: Most of the time yes, but sometimes there can be minor disturbances that don't come out as seizures or epileptic fits that can affect children's behavior.

SECTION E: **Lead Poisoning**

QUESTION: What else can show the symptoms of ADD or Hyperactivity?

ANSWER: Lead Poisoning

QUESTION: How in the 1990's can children still get lead poisoning?

ANSWER: We've seen a number of children at the Center during the last couple of years who have had lead poisoning. One family lived in a house that had been built at the turn of the century and when their child was small he was chewing on paint. This is the "old traditional" way to get lead poisoning. Two other children we saw got lead poisoning from pottery that their parents had brought home with them from vacation in Guatemala and somewhere in Europe. Sometimes in foreign countries, pottery is still made with lead-based paints.

Lead poisoning remains a problem in the 1990's. Today, approximately one in six children in America have high levels of lead in their blood. This fact is according to the Agency for Toxic Substances and Disease Registry.

Some ways to guard against lead poisoning are as follows:

1.   Do not store food or any type of liquid in any type of imported pottery, old pottery, or lead crystal.

2.   If you reuse plastic bags to store food, make sure the printing is on the outside of the bag.

3.   If your home is an older house, it is possible for water to pick up lead from old pipes made from lead materials. Water can be tested to see if it contains toxic levels of lead. If there are high levels of lead in your water, you can purchase a filter that is certified for lead removal.

4.   Do not bring dust from lead into your home. Some jobs in construction, painting, battery work, radiator repair work, and lead factories involve working with lead. It is possible to bring lead dust into your home from those mentioned places or even if your hobby involves lead. Wash your hands and your children's hands before you eat. If you work in a job or have a hobby that involves lead, change your clothes before you go home. When you go home, take a shower and wash really carefully.

5.   Be careful and aware of lead paint. Prior to 1978 some homes contain lead paint. It can be dangerous if paint peels and tiny chips are eaten. Make sure your child does not chew anything covered with lead paint such as windows.

6.   Do not remove lead paint yourself. Call an expert in to do it. Some local State Health Departments will test your home for lead paint.

7.   Ordinary dust and dirt may contain lead. Children can get lead poisoning if they breathe or swallow lead contained dirt or dust.

8.   Insist that your children wash their hands before eating. Wash bottles and pacifiers if they fall on the floor. Wash children's toys regularly. In addition to eating, make sure your children wash their hands before naptime and bedtime.

9.   Children should be tested for lead. It cannot be determined if a child has lead poisoning unless he is tested. A blood test only takes a few minutes.

10.   Some homemade remedies, particularly one used in Hispanic communities for indigestion called "azarcon" and "greta" contain high amounts of lead.

11.   Do not use old, imported or handmade dishes for any type of food or drink usage unless you know for sure that they do not contain lead.

CHAPTER SIX: How To Get Your Child To Behave And Listen To You, Part I

When people come to the Center, the most frequently asked questions they have about their ADHD child are, "How do I get him to behave?" "How do I get him back in control?" "How do I get him to listen to me?" "How do I get him to stop causing problems in school?"

This section is designed to give you specific answers to your questions about how to discipline your ADHD child, get him to listen to you and get him to behave.

We suggest that parents use a really specific format and different steps in working with the challenge of their ADHD children.

QUESTION: What are the steps to take when an ADHD child breaks a rule, misbehaves, or doesn't listen?

ANSWER: STEP I: Deal with mom's anger.
STEP II: Talk to the child about his behavior and get him to acknowledge what he did wrong.
STEP III: Give a consequence.
STEP IV: Cue the child.
STEP V: Role play when appropriate to the situation.
STEP VI: The next time the child is around the same situation, rescue again.

QUESTION: Can you explain those steps in detail and give examples of how they work in practice?

ANSWER: We'll explain the steps by giving you specific examples:

Mom gets called for the sixth time in two months by her 6-year-old child's 1st grade teacher. The teacher tells her that her child repeatedly pushes other children at school. This usually happens when he's in line. He won't wait his turn and pushes to the head of the line.

STEP I: DEAL WITH MOM'S ANGER

Let's take the situation step-by-step. The first thing the mom does is see where she is with her anger. If she's really angry, it's not a good time to talk to her child. She needs to do whatever is necessary to calm down. Have a cup of coffee, read the newspaper, take 15 minutes, an hour or two hours so when she speaks to her child she is calm.

STEP II: TALK TO THE CHILD ABOUT HIS BEHAVIOR AND GET HIM TO ACKNOWLEDGE WHAT HE DID WRONG

Mom then goes up to the child and finds out what happened. She asks, "What happened at school today? The teacher called and said she was not happy with your behavior." The child may not know or he may say, "I don't know." If she can't get the information from one or two questions, she cues the child by saying, "The teacher called and said that you pushed two children today while you were standing in line." After mom tells her child what the teacher said, she states to the child, "What did you do wrong?" Mom needs the child to verbally acknowledge that he did something wrong.

STEP III: GIVE A CONSEQUENCE

In this case, an appropriate consequence may be giving the child a four minute time-out.

STEP IV: CUE THE CHILD

After the time-out, she recues. "What did you do wrong that I had to give you a time-out?" This is to get the child to acknowledge that he can't push other children and has to wait his turn in line.

STEP V: ROLE PLAY WHEN APPROPRIATE TO THE SITUATION

Mom gets four or five chairs out and puts them in front of the kitchen sink. She then puts the child at the end of the line. "OK," mom says, "We're going to practice what we've learned." Then mom makes a little game out of it where the first chair gets a drink of water. She actually takes a chair, moves it up to a pretend water fountain, lifts the chair up and gives it a drink of water. After 30 seconds, she moves the chair out of the way. She moves all of the chairs up and repeats this with each chair until her son gets a "pretend drink" after the fourth chair. She cues again, "What are you going to do tomorrow?" Mom gets the child to verbalize that he's not going to push in line.

QUESTION: What about Step VI?

ANSWER: The next time the child is around the same situation you just recue again. The best time to do this is in the morning just before the child goes to school. The mom can say, "What are you going to do today? What behavior will you watch today so that you won't get in trouble?" If the child doesn't verbalize it, the mom says, "You need to stand in line until it's your turn, and not push the other children."

27

QUESTION: What exactly is a "time-out?"

ANSWER: "Time-out" means just what it says. You take the child away from any type of stimulation or relationship. You isolate the child by putting him in an area by himself. This serves the purpose of having some adverse or negative effect on a youngster and lets him think about what he did. He's deprived of play behavior, relationships or stimulation.

QUESTION: How exactly do you give a time-out?

ANSWER: You put the child in a chair that is facing a blank wall and use a timer to measure the exact time.

QUESTION: What kind of timer?

ANSWER: You buy a kitchen timer and you set it for the exact amount of time.

QUESTION: How long should a time-out be?

ANSWER: It depends upon the age of the youngster. For a six-year-old it should be one to five minutes.

QUESTION: How about a four-year-old?

ANSWER: It shouldn't be any longer than two minutes.

QUESTION: How about for an eight- or nine-year-old?

ANSWER: For an eight- or nine-year-old the time-out should be anywhere from two to ten minutes.

QUESTION: What other consequences can you give children other than time-outs?

ANSWER: You can make them go to bed early. If they're old enough, you can make them write sentences. You can take away TV or Nintendo for a couple of hours a day. You could take away a favorite toy for a couple of hours a day.

QUESTION: What do you mean by "making a child write sentences"?

28

ANSWER: When a child is old enough to write, you make him write 25, 50, or 100 times (depending on the age of the child) a sentence such as "I won't push other children," "I won't hit my brother," "I won't ride my bicycle on the lawn."

QUESTION: What is the point of writing sentences?

ANSWER: The point is to make the consequence so adverse the negative that there is an incentive for the child not to repeat the negative behavior and receive a negative consequence.

QUESTION: When you take a toy away from a four-year-old, how long do you take it away?

ANSWER: Depending upon the punishment, if it's a mild one you can take the toy away for a couple of hours. If not all day or until the end of their nap. If it's a severe punishment take the toy away for at least a day.

QUESTION: What about a six-year-old?

ANSWER: For a six-year-old, you can take a toy away for a half a day or a whole day.

QUESTION: What about an eight or nine-year-old?

ANSWER: For an eight or nine-year-old, you might take TV or Nintendo time away for a couple of hours then for the rest of the day.

For an eight, nine or ten-year-old again you might double or triple the time to one or two days.

QUESTION: Do you ever take privileges or toys away for a week or two weeks?

ANSWER: No.

QUESTION: Why?

ANSWER: ADHD children have problems with impulse control. They act before they think. If you give them long time-outs or long punishments, they figure they can't get it back so they give up. If they give up the punishment doesn't have any value.

QUESTION: Then how do you really help them?

ANSWER: With repeated consequences, it will teach them not to have something taken away over a long period of time.

QUESTION: What if you have a situation where the mother of a four-year-old has repeatedly told him not to take books off the coffee table? The child repeatedly does this and throws them on the floor. He walks in the room and within three seconds the books are all down. Then he goes to the book shelf and takes more books out of the bookshelf. What does mom do?

ANSWER: Let's go through this step by step.

STEP I: DEAL WITH MOM'S ANGER

Mom checks for her anger. If she is angry, she does whatever he needs to do to calm down. She needs to say "Time-out." "I need time by myself." She has a cup of coffee, she reads the paper, or she watches television until she's calm.

STEP II: TALK TO THE CHILD ABOUT HIS BEHAVIOR AND GET HIM TO ACKNOWLEDGE WHAT HE DID WRONG

Mom cues the child. "What did you do wrong?" A four-year-old may or may not be able to verbalize. If she can't get him to acknowledge, she says, "You pulled the books off the shelf. Pulling the books off of the shelf was wrong. Your behavior was wrong." She gets the child to verbally acknowledge what he did wrong.

STEP III: GIVE A CONSEQUENCE

Mom gives the consequence. She helps him to put the books back on the shelf. If he refuses, she forces him to put the books back on the shelf. She puts the books in his hand and helps him put the books back on the shelf.

After mom forces him to pick up the books, she also gives him a time-out by putting him in a chair facing the wall for two minutes.

STEP IV: CUE THE CHILD

Following the time-out, mom cues him again, "What did you do wrong?" She gets him to acknowledge what he did by saying, "I pulled the books off the of the shelf."

STEP V: ROLE PLAY WHEN APPROPRIATE TO THE SITUATION

Mom then goes into role playing. She goes back into the living room with him and the books. She sits with her child on the floor or in a special place and says, "What are the rules when you are in the Living Room?" Mom makes him verbalize that he won't pull the books off the shelf. Then she finds something else for him to play with and they play with it together for a while.

STEP VI: RECUE THE NEXT TIME THE CHILD IS AROUND THE SAME SITUATION

The mom goes into the room again the next time the child is there and asks, "What are the rules when you are in the Living Room?"

QUESTION: What do you do about a seven-year-old whose dad just told him, "Don't ride your tricycle on the flowers I've planted." Dad walks away toward the house and ten seconds later the child is riding his trike on the flowers. What should the dad do?

ANSWER: STEP I: DEAL WITH THE ANGER

Deal with parental anger. Dad needs to be calm before he speaks to the child. He needs to do whatever necessary to be calm. Take a few minutes, have a cola, walk around the house and then he speaks to his son.

STEP II: TALK TO THE CHILD ABOUT HIS BEHAVIOR AND GET HIM TO ACKNOWLEDGE WHAT HE DID WRONG

"What did you do wrong?" If the child won't acknowledge it, the father looks at him and says again "What did you do wrong?" If the child still won't acknowledge it, then the father verbalizes it. "You rode your tricycle on the flowers after I told you not to."

STEP III: GIVE A CONSEQUENCE

Dad immediately gets a gardening tool out and, with the child, replants the flowers. Then he gives the child a five minute time-out. The child faces the wall and does nothing or he loses the tricycle for the remainder of the day.

STEP IV: CUE THE CHILD

"What are the rules about riding your tricycle outside?"

STEP V: ROLE PLAY WHEN APPROPRIATE

Dad then role plays. He goes back on the lawn with the child and the tricycle. He has the child ride his tricycle as he watches him for about five or seven minutes or until the child knows that he can't ride on the flowers. Dad recues again, "What are the rules about riding the tricycle outside?" He then takes the tricycle away for the day.

STEP VI: RECUE THE NEXT TIME THE CHILD IS AROUND THE SAME SITUATION

The next time the child wants to ride his trike around the flowers, the father recues again. He says, "What are the rules about riding your tricycle outside?" He gets the child to verbalize that he can't ride his trike on the flowers.

Let's take a situation of a nine-year-old boy who won't allow his five-year-old brother to play Nintendo. Mom said, "You each play one game. It's both of yours." The nine-year-old won't share. What does the mom do?

Mom stops the game immediately and turns it off. She then begins the steps.

STEP I: MOM CHECKS HER ANGER

If she's angry, she does whatever is necessary for her to calm down.

STEP II: TALK TO THE CHILD ABOUT HIS BEHAVIOR AND GET HIM TO ACKNOWLEDGE WHAT HE DID WRONG.

Mom cues her nine-year-old by asking him why he doesn't want to share or why he can't share. She asks what he did wrong and why mom is angry. Mom gets him to verbalize. She talks about the rules of sharing, and asks him to repeat them.

STEP III: GIVE A CONSEQUENCE

Many times these children don't engage in conversation so immediately. Mom gives a consequence by having the child sit in the corner, facing the wall for six minutes.

If he doesn't respond after six minutes she sends him away from the game. If he does respond, she says, "That's good."

STEP IV: CUE THE CHILD

Following the consequences she cues the child saying, "What are the rules about sharing?"

STEP V: ROLE PLAY WHEN APPROPRIATE

Mom then role plays with her son. They each practice taking two or three turns with the Nintendo.

STEP VI: RECUE THE NEXT TIME THE CHILD IS AROUND THE SAME SITUATION

The next time the boys play the game, mom recues again by saying, "What are the rules you need to follow when you and your brother are playing Nintendo?"

QUESTION: What other consequences can you give children other than time-outs?

ANSWER: What you need to do is take away things that they like, make them go to bed early, write sentences, no TV for a couple of hours a day or take away a favorite toy for a period of time.

QUESTION: How long do you take away a favorite toy?

ANSWER: It depends upon the age of the child and the severity of the problem.

QUESTION: What about a four-year-old? For how long?

ANSWER: For a four-year-old, take the toy away until after dinner or a nap.

QUESTION: What's a severe punishment for a four-year-old?

ANSWER: A severe punishment for a four-year-old would be to take the toy away for a whole day.

QUESTION: If it's a six-year-old, and a mild punishment?

ANSWER: If it's a six-year-old, you can lengthen the time. Since they understand period of time better than a younger child, take the toy away for a half a day.

QUESTION: What would be a severe punishment for a six-year-old?

33

ANSWER: For a six-year-old, a severe punishment would be to take the toy away for a period of two days at most.

QUESTION: For an eight- or nine-year-old, how long would you take it away if it were a mild punishment?

ANSWER: For something mild, you'd take the TV or Nintendo for the rest of the day, or make him go to bed early.

QUESTION: For a severe punishment for an eight- or nine-year-old, what do you do?

ANSWER: You would double or triple the amount of time.

QUESTION: Could you explain why you don't believe in long-term punishments?

ANSWER: Long-term punishments are simply not effective with ADHD children because most of these youngsters have problems with impulse control. They think that if they can't get the toy or privilege back in a reasonable amount of time, then they give up. If they give up the punishment has no value. They figure they have nothing to lose by getting into trouble again. It's the repeated consequences, the repeated taking of things away that will help them; not taking away one thing for a long period of time.

QUESTION: Why do these children continually defy their parents? You talked about the example earlier about the father who repeatedly told his son not to ride his tricycle in the flowers, yet he continued to do so.

ANSWER: There could be a number of reasons. One is that ADHD children have poor impulse control. They act before they think. Parents need to understand that their youngsters may not think things out. They may just act out. That doesn't mean that it's acceptable. What we suggest here will help with these problems.

A second reason that these types of youngsters do these things is they are generally angrier than most children. One of the hallmarks of ADHD children is they have a shorter frustration tolerance. They may act because they are angry.

They may be angry about what they had for breakfast that morning. They may be angry about something you said to them. ADHD children act before they think things through. Their anger and impulse control take over and they act out.

Parents need to accept the fact that they're different from other youngsters and react accordingly.

Parents often say, "It's like my son has a wall around his head. Nothing gets in." Or a mom will say, "He just doesn't get it. I repeat myself and repeat myself but he just doesn't understand." ADHD children take a lot more time, energy and effort. Moms sometimes feel like they have three children instead of one because of the amount of energy and time they must put into their ADHD child. The methods we suggest here work effectively with ADHD children. The secret is you must be consistent and firm.

QUESTION: Let's take the situation of an eight-year-old boy who always seems to pick on his four-year-old sister. He pushes her, he shoves her, he hits her. Actually, he's hurt her before and mom is really afraid that he could really be damaging. He fights hard and it seems really certain that the four-year-old sister is not 100% blameless. If you look at it objectively, an awful lot comes from him. What mom doesn't want to tolerate is his physical abuse of his sister.

ANSWER: Again, let's go through this step-by-step.

STEP I: DEAL WITH PARENTAL ANGER

This is one situation where mom has to respond immediately if her son is physically hurting a child. Mom needs to deal with her anger later.

STEP II: TALK TO THE CHILD ABOUT HIS BEHAVIOR AND GET HIM TO ACKNOWLEDGE WHAT HE DID WRONG

Mom immediately stops the physical act and talks to her son about why he hit his sister. She gives him a chance to explain himself. Usually, children do not have rational reasons for this type of behavior. The typical things they might say are, "Sister started it!" "Sister gets more attention!" and "It's all Sister's fault!"

STEP III: GIVE A CONSEQUENCE

The mother then tells her son, "If you hit your sister, I'll immediately put you in a time-out, make you write sentences or take away things that you enjoy."

In this case, the consequence is putting the youngster in an adverse situation; such as giving him a time-out for five minutes or making him write twenty-five sentences: "I will not hit my sister."

STEP IV: CUE THE CHILD

After the time-out is done, the mother asks the child, "Why did I put you in time-out?" She waits until the child verbalizes what he did wrong.

STEP V: ROLE PLAY WHEN APPROPRIATE TO THE SITUATION

Mom sits in the vicinity of her son and his sister. They play together and mom watches for five minutes.

STEP VI: RECUE AGAIN THE NEXT TIME THE CHILD IS AROUND THE SAME SITUATION

Before mom leaves the room, she recues again, "What aren't you going to do to your sister?"

QUESTION: Let's take a situation of a three-and-a-half-year-old girl who has temper tantrums in the supermarket. If mom doesn't buy her cookies or a Popsicle, she screams and shouts and carries on by throwing herself on the floor. Mom is afraid that people are going to arrest her for child abuse.

ANSWER: STEP I: DEAL WITH MOM'S ANGER

Mom must handle the situation right away, so she can't deal with her anger at this point. She must put it on the shelf and get back to it.

STEP II: TALK TO THE CHILD ABOUT HIS BEHAVIOR AND GET HIM TO ACKNOWLEDGE WHAT HE DID WRONG

Mom takes the child aside and calmly tells her, "I'm not going to give you what you want." Then mom goes to the check-out stand letting the child cry and scream. Mom repeats softly, "You're not going to get what you want." She checks out her groceries and leaves.

When mom leaves the store with the child, she says, "You cannot do that to me in a store. If you do this again, I'll leave the store and I won't take you with me next time I go to the store." Mom says again, "You will not be allowed to yell and scream and you will have to sit in the time-out chair when we get home."

STEP III: GIVE A CONSEQUENCE

Mom gives the child a consequence by having a time-out in the car, by sitting quietly in the seat for three minutes.

If the child continues her tantrum, mom can take her home and give a consequence there by giving her a time-out for two minutes.

STEP IV: CUE THE CHILD

Mom recues by asking the child, "What can you not do in the supermarket?" A three-and-a-half- year-old may not be able to verbalize that completely, but mom insists that the child answer, "I can't have cookies, and I can't scream when you say no."

STEP V: ROLE PLAY WHEN APPROPRIATE TO THE SITUATION

At this point, if mom isn't at home, she then goes home and does role playing there. She takes cookies and other treats from the shelf, and places them by the child. They pretend they have a shopping cart at the supermarket and the child cannot take anything without asking her mom.

STEP VI: RECUE THE NEXT TIME THE CHILD IS AROUND THE SAME SITUATION

If possible, mom should return to the supermarket again that afternoon or evening while the situation is still fresh in the child's memory. Mom should only pick up a couple of items so that if the child acts out she can immediately pick up the child and walk out of the supermarket.

Upon arrival at the supermarket, mom asks the child, "What can you not do while in the market?" Mom is actually going back to the supermarket to control the youngster's behavior and test whether or not the youngster can control herself in the store.

QUESTION: What happens if I do all of these things that you've discussed and it doesn't work?

ANSWER: That's the time you need to come in for short-term counseling. At the Center, we specialize in ADHD children and other problems such as Oppositional-Defiant Disorder, Organicity, or Early Childhood Trauma. We work with parents and children by helping parents learn how to control their children. We use strictly behavioral therapy, which means

we teach parents and children cause and effect. We teach parents how to get back into control.

ADHD children are extremely complicated and difficult. If the methods suggested in this information guide don't work, then it's time to get what we call "coaching." "Coaching" means learning special skills to parent an ADHD child.

There is nowhere you can go to learn how to be a parent of an ADHD child.

There are classes offered to learn how to play racquetball, cook Chinese food, garden, or speak a foreign language. However, I have never heard of a place you can go to learn how to be an ADHD parent. We simply give you the tools, methods and techniques necessary to get your child back into control and to obey your rules.

One way to explain the "coaching" we do in counseling sessions is to compare it to your child having a toothache. You wouldn't hesitate to take him to a dentist. Likewise, if your child had a sore throat, you wouldn't hesitate to take him to a doctor; and if your child had a broken arm, you wouldn't hesitate to take him to an orthopedic doctor. Our specialty is working with ADHD children and children with similar problems. When parents have children who don't behave, we help to teach them how to get them into control.

QUESTION: What do you do about an eight-year-old boy, who says whenever he plays with the kids in the neighborhood they pick on him? He says they call him names and they hit him and he says it is never his fault. Mom knows when she looks out the window that in 90% of the cases, it is his fault. The boy takes toys away from the other kids, he pushes them. How does she help him?

ANSWER: Let's go through the steps.

STEP I: DEAL WITH PARENTAL ANGER

If mom is really angry, she needs to take some time to cool off before she deals with him. She can say, "OK, let's talk about this in a little while." She then needs to do whatever is necessary for her to relax and calm down.

STEP II: TALK TO THE CHILD ABOUT HIS BEHAVIOR AND GET HIM TO ACKNOWLEDGE WHAT HE DID WRONG

Mom asks the boy, "What happened?" The boy tells her, "Someone else picked on me. I was playing stick hockey when, someone hit me and then they called me stupid."

STEP III: GIVE A CONSEQUENCE

This is a teaching situation where it probably would be better not to give a consequence.

STEP IV: CUE THE CHILD

Mom says, "It's really important when you play with other kids to let everyone take their turn." She goes on to explain what the rules are when they play soccer and what the boy needs to do to be part of the team.

STEP V: ROLE PLAY WHEN APPROPRIATE

Mom needs to go outside with the child and play with him alone. She takes a turn, he takes a turn, she takes a turn, he takes a turn, and so on. When the boy acts impulsively without thinking and wants to take it when it's not his turn, mom says, "No! This is what you can't do." At this point mom asks, "What did you do that will make other people angry?"

STEP VI: RECUE THE NEXT TIME THE CHILD IS AROUND THE SAME SITUATION

When the boy is ready to go back and play with the other children, mom asks him, "What do you need to do to get along with the other children?" She makes him verbalize that he needs to share and take turns.

QUESTION: Your method of "cueing" seems very cruel and mean. I don't want to subject my child to something that is cruel and mean. You seem much too harsh on children.

ANSWER: Your question about our methods being "cruel and mean" is the most frequently asked question that we receive regarding our specific methods of teaching parents how to work with their ADHD children. Some parents look at it and say it's too harsh, mean or cruel and they just won't follow through with it.

Our intent is to help children learn to obey rules at home and at school.

When children are out-of-control, they not only cause problems at home and school but ultimately it isn't good for them. They don't feel good about themselves and their self-esteem decreases. If behaviors aren't changed or corrected, they only get worse.

When ADHD children become teens, they are very susceptible to severel adolescent problems such as drugs, alcohol, running away, not going to school, dropping out of school

and being involved in criminal justice activities ranging from vandalism or shoplifting all the way to burglary and armed robbery.

QUESTION: Why are these children subject to these types of problems when they are adolescents?

ANSWER: Again, the characteristics of ADHD include difficulty concentrating and poor impulse control.

If ADHD children are not "in control" by the time they reach adolescence, the difficulty with impulse control leads them to have a hard time resisting peer group pressure. This is when they get involved with negative types of behavior such as those I've listed above.

In addition, drugs and alcohol give an immediate "soothing or feeling good." The child having difficulty with impulse control is extremely susceptible to this.

We specialize with both children and teens at our Center for Family Life Enrichment. Approximately 30% of the teens we see with severe out-of-control behaviors, such as those I've listed, have a history and background of ADHD. Most psychologists believe ADHD affects 5% to 10% of the population. You can see that the proportion of teens with an ADHD background and who are out-of-control is much higher.

That is why it is really critical to get your children to follow structure and control.

I don't see our methods as being "cruel" or "mean." I see them as being consistent, firm and strict. In more than 20 years at the Center, we've learned that these methods are really successful in helping an ADHD child.

QUESTION: I still feel that this is mean. Why can't you just reason and talk with children?

ANSWER: You can. But ADHD children are much different than "regular" children. Reasoning almost never works.

What we recommend is that you be strict, firm, set limits and keep your limits.

Another way to say this is you need to be consistent.

Every parent wants his children to be successful in every aspect of their lives; to do well in school, to have friends, to enjoy activities and to get along well with parents. The strict and firm methods we teach will enable a child to be successful in all areas of his life.

QUESTION: What do I do if all of your behavioral techniques and cueing don't work at all with my child? I notice it helping a little but it doesn't have any lasting change.

ANSWER: Each child is different. Each ADHD child is different. Many parents find these specific guidelines very helpful. However, there is a wide range of responses ADHD children have to these specific methods.

QUESTION: Why can't I do it by myself?

ANSWER: We have this information guide because we hope that you can learn this by yourself.

The question is, "What if you can't do it?" or "What if it doesn't work?"

Because each child is different, the methods used may have to be individualized and modified to help each individual child.

For example; if your child had a toothache, you wouldn't try to treat him unless you were a dentist. If your child had a sore throat, you wouldn't try to treat him unless you were a doctor, And you wouldn't try to fix your child's broken arm unless you were an orthopedic surgeon.

We would encourage you to bring your child to a counseling center that specializes in behavioral methods to help children with ADHD.

QUESTION: Will counseling help?

ANSWER: We've been working with ADHD children and their parents at our Center for more than twenty years. Parents find our methods very helpful. We believe counseling can be a great benefit.

**CHAPTER SEVEN: How To Get Your Children To Behave And Listen To You
Part II**

This Chapter will focus on some principles and give a detailed explanation of how to get your children to behave and listen to you.

ADHD children need a family that's highly structured. They need a family where the rules of the house are posted and clearly understood. ADHD chlidren should know what the consequences will be if they break the rules.

The family and parents need to be consistent in applying these rules.

QUESTION: What does that mean? What, specifically, do parents need to do?

ANSWER: Here are 10 key things that parents need to do:

1.   Post the rules in the family room, the child's bedroom, the kitchen and the dining room.

      ADHD children need constant reminders of the rules. People process information in two major ways. The first is auditory in which they hear information and auditorily "absorb" the information. The second major way people process information is visually in which they see things and process the information through their visionary sensory pathways.

      When parents continually remind and tell ADHD children of the rules, they are only using the child's auditory processing methodology. By posting rules and continually pointing to the rules, parents are also using their child's visual processing methodology.

2.   When your child doesn't obey a rule, go to the chart and point to the rule. Tell him, "This is a rule you need to follow." If your child doesn't know how to read, read it to him. "If you continue to break this rule, there will be a consequence." Tell him what the consequence will be; whether it's a time-out or taking a privilege away such as the TV or Nintendo.

3.   Set up a signal to cue your child. For example, when tugging at your ear. That cue will mean he's misbehaivng. Then point to something on the chart. If your child doesn't read yet, point to something on the chart and tell him the rule that he is breaking.

4. ADHD children do best with a regular routine. Make lists of everything that must be done every night along with the times.

   For example, "9:00: Turn off TV. 9:02: Change into pajamas. 9:15: Brush teeth. 9:20: Lay out school clothes for next day. 9:30: Say good-night to mom and dad. 9:40: Turn off lights and lay in bed."

   Parents need to check on their children to make sure they have completed each item on the list.

   Parents also need to make a similar list of all of the things the child needs to do each morning.

   For example, "7:00: Alarm wakes him up. 7:05: Take a shower. 7:15: Get dressed. 7:25: Make lunch. 7:35: Eat breakfast. 7:50: Check homework and put it and lunch in school bag."

   Schedule the time for the child. Schedule what time the TV goes off at night before bedtime. Schedule what time he has to brush his teeth. Schedule what time he is to get into bed. Schedule what time the lights have to be turned out and he has to be laying down. Schedule what time he has to get up in the morning. Schedule what time he has to brush his teeth. Schedule what time he needs to be dressed. Schedule what time he needs to be downstairs for breakfast.

5. When a child is old enough, have him bring a homework assignment home each day, have him write down his assignment and have the teacher initial it. After mom or dad goes over each assignment, they and the child initial it and the homework sheet is returned to school.

6. Don't put your child in situations where you know he is sure to fail. If you are shopping one day and want to go into a china and glass shop, don't take your child. Go back to the store when your child is not with you.

   If your child has had a really bad day and you need to go to the grocery store and your child has problems in the grocery store, don't take him. If you are single mom, don't go to the grocery store. If you desperately need an item, see if you can borrow it from a neighbor or go without it.

If you are going over to your sister's house and you know that your ADHD child has a lot of conflicts with his cousins, give the children a break from each other after ten or fifteen minutes together.

Have the children watch a video on the VCR and you sit between them so that they can't kick or annoy each other.

7. Whenever you see your child getting worked up or over-stimulated, withdraw him from the situation. For example; if you are watching him on the playground and you get a sense that he is going to push another child, walk up and tell him, "We're going to take a break now."

When you see your child getting worked up or over-stimulated, this is the time to use your cueing signals like tugging your ear, or whatever signal you have arranged with your child.

8. Mornings seem to be a real problem for ADHD children. It is hard to get them to follow your regularly planned schedule and you are always in a rush. The best way to solve this problem is to get up twenty minutes earlier so you and your child are not as rushed.

Particularly for smaller children (three-, four- or five-year-olds), the things that we take for granted in the mornings like getting up, becoming alert, making your bed, brushing your teeth, washing your face, taking a shower, getting dressed, making sure your clothes are adjusted and on straight, buttoning your clothes, using zippers, putting on socks and shoes, getting your lunch into your school bag and putting other things into your school bag can be an awful lot to do and overwhelming for an ADHD child.

Parents who have adopted our theory of getting up twenty minutes earlier say they are amazed at how much easier their mornings are when every second doesn't count and they have a little bit more time to remind their child to do the chores he needs to do to get ready.

CHAPTER EIGHT: Dealing With Mom's Anger

When moms come into our office, I always know if they have an ADHD child because they look exhausted. I'm being only half facetious.

I've often said that I wouldn't wish an ADHD on my worst enemy, if I had one. The best way to describe the behavior of these children is "exhausting."

It seems that instead of one child, you're raising three to four children. It takes as much work and energy to raise three to four "regular" children as it does one ADHD child. These children don't ever stop. They're always in motion.

Moms are exhausted. They feel frustrated, drained and tired. It doesn't ever stop. It just goes on and on and on.

QUESTION: What can a mother do with her anger?

ANSWER: ADHD children represent an incredible challenge. Parents first need to realize that this is a genetic problem; it's inherited like eye or hair color. Parents shouldn't blame themselves. Very often the ADHD parents blame themselves. This is also a problem that requires an enormous amount of time and energy on the part of the parent.

The more positive, assertive, consistent and active you are the quicker these behaviors will go away. A parent needs to accept that their child is ADHD and that his behavior is going to be different from that of an average child. They may have to put in three times the amount of time with an ADHD child than an average child. But in the end it will be OK. The extra time will result in better behavior, more self-esteem for the child and less anger and frustration for the parent.

If a child had a physical illness, such as a long-term physical problem that required a parent to change bandages on his arms and legs every hour, it would be very frustrating and use a lot of energy but you would accept the fact that you needed to help the child.

With that as a background, this Chapter on "anger" is divided into three sections: General Background, the Angry Parent and the Angry Child.

This first section deals with anger as a general subject and gives you the background you need to understand your anger and your child's anger.

1. GENERAL BACKGROUND

Anger is a necessary, productive and healthy feeling. Our problem in the past has been that we tried to stifle angry feelings or we dealt with these feelings in ways that were destructive and/or counterproductive.

When feelings of anger are constantly stifled, both physical and mental health deteriorate. Anger is an energy that must find some outlet. If we deny ourselves that outlet, this same energy starts to consume us. If we allow ourselves to express these angry feelings inappropriately, in a destructive or counterproductive way, we are left with the additional problems of guilt.

We live in a complicated, complex, industrialized society and there are a lot of situations both inside and outside our family that make us angry everyday. In addition, because of the nature of the problem, the mom of an ADHD child will get angry even more often than the ordinary person. A person who is dealing with his anger in a constructive way will usually admit to getting angry as many as three to five times a day, if not more.

Very often it is inappropriate to carry out the action that comes to mind with the feelings, but remember that no matter how violent your thoughts, it's OKAY to have your THOUGHTS. It is NOT OKAY to carry out the ACTIONS.

Let's take an example: A woman is driving on the freeway and suddenly a car swerves into her lane of traffic and only by slamming on her brakes and skidding for a couple of hundred feet is she able to avoid a serious accident. Right at that moment she feels so angry at the driver of the other car she would like to ram her car into his. Again, there is absolutely nothing wrong with feeling that amount of anger. It is normal, appropriate and healthy. What WOULD be wrong would be to ram her car into the other driver's car.

Experience your angry feelings with as much intensity as you want and allow yourself an action-thought to fit your feeling; but don't act out or feel guilty about those action-thoughts.

Understanding your anger and expressing it in a healthy manner is crucial to your relationship with your child. It is important that you provide a role model showing him how to handle anger and it is important that you and your child have a healthy give-and-take relationship between you.

2.   THE ANGRY CHILD

The ADHD child experiences a lot of frustration in his life. Much more than the average child. He gets criticized and yelled at when he is at school, home or playing and doing activities. The anger becomes cumulative and he feels it more and more.

Here are some ways you can help your ADHD child (or any child) deal with his anger:

Explain to your child that having anger is OK and that there are good and bad ways to deal with it. Bad ways are calling names, hitting, or throwing things.

An example of good ways to deal with anger would be to place the child on his bed and tell him, "When you're angry, come in here and take your pillow (you actually role play with him) and hit it on the bed and tell yourself this is mom, this is dad, this is one of your friends." Teach him to discharge his anger that way.

Another example of a good way to deal with anger would be to give the child a towel. This would be his "angry towel." Whenever he gets angry, he twists the towel and tells himself out loud if he wants that this is his mother he's twisting, or his father, his brother, his sister, or his teacher. You've now given him constructive ways to discharge his anger.

3.   THE ANGRY PARENT

Because of the nature and challenge of ADHD children, parents often become very angry with them.   Parents need to specifically work off their anger in ways that we've discussed before: 1. Talk to someone such as your husband or friend. 2. You can hit the bed with your pillow or twist a towel. 3. Do some type of sporting activity such as jogging, playing tennis or golf. Any of these things are examples of how to discharge your anger.

It's important for both parents and children to develop these mechanisms so anger doesn't build up and gets dissipated as soon as possible.

CHAPTER NINE: **How To Get Your Child To Go To Sleep**

QUESTION: What do you do about a five-and-a-half-year-old child who just won't go to sleep? This child will not take naps and he gets up at 5:30 every morning. He is a little whirlwind until 11:30 at night.

ANSWER: Not taking naps is typical ADHD behavior. This is what you need to do to work with your child:

First, you need to set a specific bedtime for him to have and stick by it every evening. Let's say you go to bed at 10:15 p.m. You go in to the child's bedroom with him and read him a story. You tell him you can't stay up all night with him. You tell the child, "This is bedtime. You may not be sleepy but the rest of us are." If you can't sleep, you can do quiet things. You can read, write, draw or color. You cannot have the TV on, leave your room or do anything else that might disturb the rest of the family." You tell the child, "If you break any of the rules like having the TV on, walking around the house or not being quiet you will get a consequence." Then you leave the room.

More likely than not, the child will break your rule. You will need to give him a consequence. The consequence should be that the child be confined to his bedroom with the lights turned off so that he cannot do anything.

To enforce that, you will probably have to sit up with him until he goes to bed. This will probably make the child very angry but you need to sit with him and wait it out. You need to make it more adverse for him to stay up and cause trouble than to stay in his room and stay quiet or fall asleep. If you make it tougher for the child to stay up and cause trouble then it is to fall asleep, he will eventually stop.

You will need to repeat this entire process evening after evening until the child follows your rules and goes to sleep.

QUESTION: How would this work with the steps?

ANSWER: You've read the child a story, and told him he needs to play quietly in his room and you go into your room. Twenty minutes later you hear him banging his toy drum and singing loudly.

STEP I: DEAL WITH PARENTAL ANGER

You immediately need to work with the child and deal with your anger later.

STEP II: **TALK TO THE CHILD ABOUT HIS BEHAVIOR AND GET HIM TO ACKNOWLEDGE WHAT HE DID WRONG**

You ask the child, "What did you do wrong?" If the child doesn't acknowledge what he did wrong you tell him, "You cannot make noise after I've told you it's bedtime."

STEP III: **GIVE A CONSEQUENCE**

The consequence in this case would be to turn off all of the lights and sit with the child on his bed until he falls asleep.

STEP IV: **CUE THE CHILD**

As the child is getting tired mom asks, "What do you need to do at bedtime?" If the child won't repeat it tell him, "Play quietly."

STEP V: **ROLE PLAY WHEN APPROPRIATE**

Mom role plays the situation the next evening. She goes to the child's room before the bedtime story and says, "OK, we're just going to practice what you can do." Mom plays with him for a few minutes while the child plays quietly with toys, draws or colors.

STEP VI: **RECUE THE NEXT TIME THE CHILD IS AROUND THE SAME SITUATION**

After mom has read the child a story, she asks him, "What are you going to do now?" And "what can't you do?"

CHAPTER TEN: Self-Esteem

The essential building block to happy, well-adjusted children is self-esteem. The ADHD child almost always has poor self-esteem. Good self-esteem comes from four major areas: 1) Love, approval and praise by parents. 2) Being successful in school. 3) Having friends, being liked and liking other people. 4) Doing well in sports and activities. The ADHD child generally has severe problems in all four of these areas.

PARENTAL APPROVAL: Because of the nature of the problem, ADHD children are almost always testing rules, pushing parents' buttons, breaking rules, getting into mischief and doing all the things that they are not supposed to do. Parents need to appropriately set limits and discipline. The parent usually feels frustrated, unhappy, angry and much less likely to compliment the child. ADHD children get a lot less support, compliments, love and nourishment. Simply the nature of who they are leads to the reaction they get from their parents.

SCHOOL BEHAVIOR: Attention Deficit Disorder is a problem of having difficulty with concentration and Hyperactivity is a problem of poor impulse control. These two traits lead most ADHD children into problems at school where they have a great deal of difficulty concentrating. They don't pay attention. The ADHD child frequently interrupts the teacher, pushes other children in line, calls out in class, fidgets, moves and walks around the room. The teacher has to spend more time disciplining them and working with these children than the other children. The ADHD child gets the idea instilled that he doesn't learn as well, that there may be something wrong with him and he thinks he's stupid. Certainly, he doesn't do well in school. He's in trouble with teachers and he keeps getting punishments and consequences so he doesn't acquire good self-esteem from that part of his life.

PEERS: Again, because of the nature of the ADHD child, he acts without thinking. He often has a hard time sharing and it's very hard for him to make friends. Most children don't like other children who pull toys away from them and push them or don't share well. Consequently, these children have very few friends so they don't acquire self-esteem in this area either.

ACTIVITIES: In sports and activities, with the nature of the ADHD child preventing him from sharing well and causing him to be impatient, he has a hard time being successful at activities. In team sports such as Little League or AYSO soccer ADHD children are frequently in trouble with the coaches because they interrupt, they push other children and they don't take their turn or listen and follow directions.

QUESTION: Knowing all of these things, how do we as parents work on building the ADHD child's self-esteem?

ANSWER: Let's look at all four of the areas and find out what the parents can do to help their ADHD child's self-esteem.

Self-esteem comes from a large number of areas. The first place it comes from is the child's or teen's feeling that they're special to their parent. Every child or teen needs to feel that they're a very unique, special person. They need to feel loved for being themselves and for their own special uniqueness and individuality.

The second place self-esteem comes from is school. We have enormous pressure from society to do well in school, to achieve in academics and activities. Children who do well in school and activities gain a lot of self-esteem.

A third way that children gain self-esteem is from having friends, being liked by friends and establishing strong relationships with peers. For children and teens, self-esteem can also come from their peers.

Fourth, self-esteem is also gained through participation and success in activities outside of school. (Any type of sport such as football, soccer, volleyball, basketball, Little League, youth group; any type of activity with Cub Scouts, Boy Scouts, Recreation Departments; any type of lessons such as piano, music, computer, or art.) It also comes from having part-time jobs. Self-esteem can also be gained from being responsible around the house and from doing chores.

When children and teens do well they feel good about themselves. It builds self-esteem. This is equally valid from the time kids are very small through their teenage years.

In addition, it's also critical and crucial that children feel love, acceptance and praise from their parents. They need to feel "special" to their parents.

Everyone has certain biological needs. We have a need to sleep a certain amount of time each night, keep our body temperature at 98.6 degrees all of the time (or pretty close to it) to take in food, water and to eliminate waste products. If we don't get these biological needs met our body goes into crisis. If the biological depravation or lack of meeting the need is severe enough, then we literally die.

In addition to biological needs, we have psychological needs.

To build good self-esteem, every child needs to feel he's special and unique to his parents. To feel special and unique to the parent is a need that's just as real as a biological need is to sleep X amount of hours a night, to take in food or to drink water.

The parents' interaction is critical to helping their child feel special. Parents need to spend time with their children. They need to praise them. They need to value them. They need to listen to them and they need to let them know through their words and actions that they are special.

We have a really special format that will help you praise your child and build his self-esteem. Research at the Center shows that the average parent gives their child one half of a compliment a week. That's not a compliment per day or a half a compliment per day. It's a half of a compliment per week!

Give your children at least one compliment per day. If you do that, you'll be giving fourteen times better than the national average.

The following are some examples of compliments that you can give to your children:

You can tell your six-year-old son you're proud of his art piece. When he brings a piece of paper back from first grade say, "Wow! That's a great drawing! I'm really proud of you! You did real well!"

You can tell your nine-year-old daughter, "Thanks for cleaning the dishes up so promptly tonight."

You can tell your twelve-year-old stepson, "Boy, you look sharp today. I really like your shirt."

You can give children compliments about their behavior, their looks, their achievements and just about themselves.

QUESTION: That sounds so easy and simple. Why don't parents give their children compliments very often?

ANSWER: That's a very good question. The first answer is that parents may not know that it's an important skill and that their children need it.

Almost all of us learn our parenting skills from our own parents. If our own parents didn't give compliments, we didn't know or learn that it was important.

In talking with thousands and thousands of parents, we've found that very few of their parents gave a lot of compliments and they also give very few compliments. They never learned that it's something you need to do.

As I've said previously, it's simple and easy. Give your children at least one compliment per day. You'll be doing fourteen times better than the national average and you'll be building your children's self-esteem.

QUESTION: Are there any other reasons why parents don't compliment their children?

ANSWER: Most people, whether they work inside the house or outside the house, work really hard. Most of us are busy with our children, our work, keeping track of the children, the house, chores, worried about money, being busy with activities and friends and spouses. So, it's really easy to forget.

Particularly since we're not in the habit of it, it's hard to break old habits of not complimenting our children and then incorporate a new habit in our behavior.

QUESTION: What do you do if you want to do this but you just kind of "forget?" You want to incorporate it into your behavior.

ANSWER: The best thing to do is to buy an inexpensive notebook at the store and keep it by your bed. Every single night write down compliments you gave to your child. If you don't do it, this will serve as a reminder to give compliments the following day.

QUESTION: What other reasons are there for parents not complimenting their children?

ANSWER: The single major reason parents of ADHD children don't compliment their children is that they are angry with them. ADHD children don't obey the rules and they are challenging and difficult. Parents often say, "It's like parenting seven children and all I have is one. I just can't get him to do anything at any time." Parents feel exhausted and their anger increases because nothing they do works for the child and things are difficult all of the time for them.

QUESTION: Are you saying it's natural to be angry at your ADHD child all of the time?

ANSWER: I'm saying that parents are under a lot of pressure and stress. Everyone; whether you work in the home or out of the home, moms and dads are really busy between working, doing family chores, parenting and all of the other activities and interests they're involved in.

The ADHD child is such a challenge and presents such difficulties at home and at school. Parents frequently tell us they are angry with their child all of the time.

Parents, if they're honest, will say things like, "I wish this child was never born," "I wish I never had this child," "I wish he would run away," "I wish I could run away." Those feelings are OK. It's a reflection on how difficult it is to manage an ADHD child.

I've often thought that there's no difference whether you work in the house or out of the house; you work really hard. When you come home, you're really tired. Very few people have "cushy" jobs. Most people spend a really long, hard day at work and come home exhausted. There's nothing I know that's a harder job than being a parent of an ADHD child, preteen or teen. So, when people walk in the door after work exhausted, the hardest job in the world begins. That job being the parent of an ADHD child, preteen or teen.

QUESTION: Let's go back to giving a child a compliment. Is it as simple as it sounds? You just say something that you like about the child? Could you give us some more examples?

ANSWER: Let's take some different ages and hear examples for each of them. For a six-year- old daughter: "Gee, you look nice in that dress today." "Thank you for hanging your jacket up without being reminded." "I love you."

For a seven-year-old son: "I'm really proud you did that great drawing at school." "You really kicked two good goals in your soccer practice." "Thank you for taking your dishes to the sink after dinner."

For an eight-year-old daughter: "When you practiced the piano, it sounded really good." "I really like that new sweater on you." "Your hair looks great today."

For a nine-year-old boy: "I'm really pleased you did so well on the test today." "You look great in that new sweatshirt." "Thank you for keeping your radio down so your brother could go to sleep."

For a ten-year-old girl: "You pick really nice friends. I really like Susie and Judy." "I appreciate your being ready to go when I pick you up at your friend's house." "Thank you for calling me right away at work when you come home from school."

For an eleven-year-old boy: "I was watching you in the yard. You really shot a lot of great baskets." "Thanks for helping set the table for supper." "Those shorts look really good on you."

For a thirteen-year-old daughter: "That's a really neat puzzle you made in school." "You look great in that skirt and blouse." "Thanks for taking care of your brother today. I really needed your help."

For a fourteen-year-old son: "You're incredible with the Nintendo. I can't believe you scored so high. "Thanks for washing the car today. I didn't have time to do it." "I'm really proud of you when you do so well on your math test."

For a fifteen-year-old daughter: "Thanks for understanding that we didn't have the money for you to go to Disneyland next week." "Thanks for helping with the vacuuming." "You did really great at your band practice today. The teacher called and told me and I'm really proud of you."

QUESTION: How often should you compliment your child?

ANSWER: If you give at least one compliment a day, it will be doing fourteen times better than the national average. I would suggest parents give their children one to two compliments a day.

QUESTION: Can you give your children too many compliments?

ANSWER: Sure, if I want to have dessert late in the evening and it's two scoops of chocolate ice cream and some syrup, I'm going to get a tummy ache. You can give a child too many compliments. If you give your child too many compliments every day, he could think that the whole world centers around himself and become really self-centered and narcissistic.

QUESTION: What do you do if you have a child who seemingly doesn't respond well to compliments and just shrugs them off?

ANSWER: You may be dealing with a child who doesn't like himself and has poor self-esteem. When you give him a compliment he just can't take it in because his self-esteem is so poor. With this type of child, he may think that you're "dumb and stupid" because if you really knew him you couldn't possibly think he deserved a compliment or he's just being a con artist and faking you out.

QUESTION: How do you give a child like that a compliment?

ANSWER: With that type of child, you praise his behavior. You don't tell a child like that, "I'm really proud you're my son," or "I really love you a lot." You praise something very

specific that he did. "Thanks for taking the trash out so promptly." "I'm really proud of you because you got a B+ on that paper. I know how hard English is for you."

QUESTION: It sounds like this is just a real simple skill in love and support.

ANSWER: Yes, this is one of the basic skills that we encourage parents to use to build a child's self-esteem; since self-esteem; is so important.

QUESTION: I've done what you recommended for three weeks now and it seems to make no difference in my child's behavior.

ANSWER: Please re-read the chapter on the importance of "Self-Esteem." It's as basic a need as eating, drinking or sleep. Your child does need it.

Mother's often tell me, "It seems like he's got a wall around his brain and doesn't take anything in."

When you give your child a compliment, look him in the eye. Make sure that you and he have eye contact and tell him the compliment. After a period of time, the compliments will start helping with your child's self-esteem.

I know it can be really discouraging. I suggest you consider an old Chinese proverb, "The journey of a thousand miles begins with the first step."

CHAPTER ELEVEN: School Problems

QUESTION: What do you do when mom gets a call from her six-year-old son's teacher at school? The teacher tells her, "He can't sit still, he doesn't seem to be able to concentrate, he's always walking around the room and he doesn't pay attention. He simply refuses to stay in his seat."

ANSWER: The first thing mom needs to do is get more information. She needs to know if this is a one-time occurrence or does he do this everyday? Mom talks to the teacher and is told this behavior goes on every single day. The teacher tells her that the child literally can't sit still for more than five or six minutes at a time.

Mom needs to pay attention (although she probably already knows) to whether he is the same way at home. Does he fidget? Does he move around a lot? In almost all of these cases mom will confirm that he displays the same behavior at home but doesn't get in trouble for it because at school you're required to sit still and concentrate.

Attention Deficit Disorder is a problem of difficulty with concentration. Hyperactivity is a problem of impulse control.

If an adult tried to fly by flapping his arms, he couldn't physiologically do it.

For a child with ADD, physiologically, it's extremely hard for him to concentrate in school. A child with Hyperactivity acts before he thinks. It's hard for him to sit still and not fidget.

If a child had poor vision, you would get him eye glasses. If your child had poor hearing, you would have his hearing checked out. If a child had juvenile diabetes, you would get him treatment and probably need to give him insulin.

At this point, the child is showing symptoms of ADHD. The best possible thing the parent can do is take him to a counselor to get him evaluated and get him professional help with his problems.

QUESTION: If I take my child to a counselor, what happens next?

ANSWER: At our Center we specialize in children, preteens and teens with ADD. The first step we take is to get the background information from the mother.

We ask her questions about her child, his behavior, and his psychological and medical history.

QUESTION: What type of questions do you ask the mother?

ANSWER: We have a 25-page questionnaire filled with more than 100 questions that ask specifics about the child's past and present personal and family history. We want to know everything about the child's prenatal history, the delivery, and the developmental history. How old he was when he held up his head, rolled over, sat alone, crawled, babbled, walked, said words and sentences. We want to know everything about his behavioral history, his moods and his temperament. We also want to know everything about his history that would lead us to believe he has ADHD. We need to know his strengths and abilities as well as his medical history. We ask all about the family history. For example; Is there a history of ADHD in the family? We also ask for any comments that the parents would like to make.

We also want to know how the mom is doing. Most of the time we find that moms are exhausted.

QUESTION: What's next?

ANSWER: What we'll suggest in most cases is to do some neuropsychological testing to find out if the child has ADHD or any other problem.

QUESTION: What is Neuropsychological testing?

ANSWER: A Neuropsychologist has had extensive training and background in dealing with these types of problems. They administer specialized tests that can determine if a child has ADHD or has any other type of problem that could be causing these behaviors.

QUESTION: What tests does a Neuropsychologist give?

ANSWER: Once we get the background from the mom, the Neuropsychologist will design a specific set of tests for that individual child. In 99% of the cases, a child is given the TOVA. The TOVA is a very simple test. The children sit in front of a computer and they hold a microswitch button which is a little button that's attached to the computer with a cord. Every time they see a black square with a white box in the upper half, they press the microswitch button. Every time they see a black square box with a white box in the lower half, they don't press the microswitch button. That's the entire test. It lasts about 22 minutes.

The TOVA measures how children pay attention. It measures impulsivity.

The impulsivity is assessed by how many times a child presses the button when he shouldn't. It also measures reaction time to a thousandth of a second and it measures how this reaction time varies; which is a measure of consistency.

It turns out that the consistency measure is the most important measure in terms of diagnosing ADHD. Next is reaction time and the third most important variable is inattention or leaving things out.

QUESTION: What's after that?

ANSWER: After that, we usually recommend short-term counseling to help the child.

QUESTION: What is short-term counseling?

ANSWER: The average family comes eight times. They come in with their child for counseling once a week for forty-five minutes. They learn specific behavioral techniques that will help them get their child to listen and obey.

CHAPTER TWELVE: The ADHD Child And The School System

If I said to you, "Please stand up and flap your arms. I'm going to teach you how to fly by flapping your arms," You could not do it. Physiologically, you are not capable of it.

ADHD children, physiologically, have great difficulties learning in school because of the nature of their disorder.

ADHD is a physiological problem with concentration, having poor impulse control and excess motor activity.

By nature of the definition of ADHD, these children are gong to have a lot of problems in the school system.

The most frequent reason parents come to our office is because their child has problems with school. Frequently, the child has been kicked out of one, two or three preschools and Kindergarten. Frequently, the parent has repeatedly heard that his child is doing poorly in preschool, Kindergarten, first and second grades. The parents have been called in by the teacher for numerous conferences and told that their child hits other children. The parents have been told that their child "just doesn't get it." Their child just sits in class and isn't learning.

We have parents tell us that the teacher doesn't like their child and is punitive or is being unfair to their child.

QUESTION: So what does a mother do when she learns that her child repeatedly has the problems with school that you've mentioned or feels that her child "isn't getting it" because the teacher says he's lazy. But, after reading all of your material, the parent suspects there may be an Attention Deficit problem?

ANSWER: When parents bring children with ADHD to us, we recommend general guidelines for helping the child with school. We work on individual guidelines for your child and we confer with the teacher based on the following:

1. Any parent can look at the guidelines and, based on his knowledge of his child, think of which ones would make more sense for that individual child. Once you have some concrete suggestions, you could go to your child's teacher and talk to him about the specific guidelines and ask for his help in implementing them with your child.

    Seat the child in the first row from the teacher's desk right in front of the teacher.

This is crucial and important. The ADHD child, if seated in the first row from the teacher, is less likely to be distracted by other students, other stimuli, and is in a position to absorb and learn better.

2. Seat two very good students on the child's left and right so that the child will have two positive role models.

   Children can learn from other children. Having two very good students sit on either side of the child can help the ADHD child learn through positive examples. The child will be able to see how the other children study, organize, and listen to the teacher. This is a very positive experience for an ADHD child.

3. Give each child at least one assignment each day in which the child can be successful and do well.

   By the nature of the child's problem, the ADHD child fails so much everyday, both at school and at home. It is really important for the child's self- esteem that the child be given one assignment each day in which the child can succeed and receive praises from the teacher. The teacher can design a specific assignment that is uncomplicated and a "lock-in guarantee" that the child can do it well and receive praise.

4. Make eye contact with the child before calling him or before giving him instructions.

   Children process information in two major ways. One is visually through their eyes and the other is auditorially through their ears. All children and adults use both of these methods to process information. Most people, including children, have a primary source; whether it is auditory or visual. By making eye contact, this gives two methods for the child to absorb information; both visually and auditory means. Eye contact also gets the child to attend to the matter for which the teacher is calling on the child.

5. Use a child's first name before calling the child.

   This is another method of cueing a child to attend to what the teacher is saying.

6. At all costs, try to avoid asking the child a question when the child is not paying attention or not in a position to respond to you (he's misbehaving). This will only embarrass the child.

Again, so much of the ADHD child's day at school and at home is negative time and attention. The goal is to avoid doing anything additional that will give the child a sense of failure or give the child negative attention. If a child is not paying attention or is "goofing-off," the child is not going to respond to you and get into more trouble.

7. Develop a cue with the child such as tugging at your ear. Meet with the child privately before class to explain the cue. Also, explain to the child that when the child goes off-task, this will be the method you will use to cue the child to get back on-task. This will be the child's secret signal from you when the child is off-task or getting lost.

A really effective way to work with an ADHD child is to cue. On a technical basis, it works by becoming a matter of conditioning. Using the conditioning theory, there is cause and effect and cause and effect. The cue is almost an unconscious methodology for the child to understand that he needs to get back on task.

8. Give the hardest academic classes in the mornings. Children are the most attentive in the mornings whether they are ADHD children or not. They do their best learning then.

9. Make sure the classroom is enclosed with four walls.

ADHD children need structure. The four walls are very important for their sense of space.

10. Display all of the classroom rules on a board in front of the class.

ADHD children need constant cueing and reminding.

11. Put the daily schedule and homework assignments in the same place everyday. Also tape a copy of the schedules on the desk of the ADHD child.

Again, ADHD children need constant cueing and reminding.

12. Give very clear directions when you go from one subject to the next activity, give real clear directions. Each time you are going to switch, announce it to the class five minutes before. For example; "You have five minutes left for your writing exercise. At the end of five minutes we are going to do math." Then announce when there are only two minutes left.

ADHD children always work better with structure.

13. If there are other children with problems, seat them as far away from the ADHD child as possible.

   The goal is to remove negative stimuli and poor role models from ADHD children.

14. Provide a quiet workplace in the classroom which would be available to any student upon request. Or you can send the child there if the child's behavior is causing problems.

   This can be a desk, a couple of desks or even a spot on the floor at the back of the room where the ADHD child can be sent if he is getting off-task or out-of-control. It can also be a place that an ADHD child can request to be sent.

15. Allow the child to stand by his desk and do his work if he child requests it.

   Because of the nature of ADHD, children have excess energy and impulsivity. Physiologically, they just can't sit still. Standing by his desk is a very good method to allow the child to dissipate the excessive motor activity.

   Allowing the child to stand by his desk, stand or walk from place to place or move a couple of feet discharges activity and still allows the child to attend to task.

16. Reduce the amount of homework given according to the child's needs.

   Each child is an individual. The teacher needs to work with each child based on the child's needs.

17. Allow more time for the child to complete assignments according to the child's needs.

   Again, each child is an individual and needs to have work from the child's teacher based on those needs.

18. Allow the child to use a computer for written assignments if the child has poor handwriting or wants to use the computer.

   The ADHD child continually needs extra stimulation. Computers work great since they will stimulate the child.

19. When the child is feeling overwhelmed, allow him to go into the quiet area to get some space and relax.

   The ADHD child can get overwhelmed quickly. The quiet space in the room will allow him to recoup.

It's really important to give ADHD children a lot of positive reinforcement. Different ways to accomplish this are to praise a child when he does well, give him jobs such as wiping off the blackboard or give extra free time.

We know that ADHD children go off-task when:

1. Their schoolwork is difficult and repetitious.
2. They have to work for long periods of time with no break.
3. The class is in a period of transition.

The teacher needs to avoid those three things by:

1. Allowing the child to go to the quiet area in the classroom when sensing, by the behavior, the child is going off-task.

2. Modify the child's assignments so that he doesn't have long periods of study.

3. Announce periods of transition at the five- and two-minute intervals..

The best way to motivate ADHD children is to give them something very action-oriented, new or stimulating to keep them away from boring or repetitious things and to give them positive attention.

QUESTION: When you call the school teachers and say you want to meet with them, are they cooperative? Do they follow the suggestions that you give them?

ANSWER: We've been doing this for fifteen years and in 99% of the cases the school teachers are very cooperative.

Most teachers today are overwhelmed with the amount of students they have. In addition to dealing with ADHD children and their behavior patterns, what's going on in society is often reflected in the other children in the classroom. The teacher's job becomes harder and harder. Universally, we find that teachers care about their students. They are committed to helping their students and they welcome suggestions on how to help a student.

When we've met with teachers, almost always they've been very receptive and have worked to implement the suggestions that we've given them.

QUESTION: What if you get a teacher who is unwilling to cooperate, won't try any of your methods or just won't work with the student?

ANSWER: Just like there are uncaring doctors, psychotherapists, psychologists or people of any other profession, we occasionally run across teachers who are not interested in using our methods.

At that point we suggest that the parents speak to the principal about putting their student in another class.

QUESTION: What else can be done?

ANSWER: The other recommendations we make frequently, based on the psychological/neuropsychological testing, is that the parents request an IEP meeting.

QUESTION: What is an IEP meeting?

ANSWER: State and Federal law mandates that if a parent requests in writing an IEP meeting, (which means Individual, Educational Planning meeting) the school district must have this meeting within a set time period; usually one month.

At that point, the parent meets with a group of school personnel who are knowledgeable in this field and have the results of the child's academic records at the school.

State and Federal law state that if a child meets certain criteria, they must be given additional help based on the child's needs.

QUESTION: Can you give an example of what an IEP meeting usually entails.

ANSWER: The IEP meeting assesses the child and, based on State and Federal law, makes recommendations as to what the academic problems are and how to help the child. For example; one plan might indicate a child should attend resource classes one period a day. Another child might go to resource classes for three or four periods a day.

QUESTION: What's a resource class?

ANSWER: Generally speaking, a resource class is a much smaller class where children receive additional help in the areas that they are weakest. Whether it's reading, handwriting, spelling or math.

QUESTION: How many children are in a resource class?

ANSWER: Anywhere from one or two, to six, eight, twelve or fifteen. So the child gets a lot more individual attention and help.

QUESTION: How long is the child in the resource class?

ANSWER: The child's performance is assessed at the end of the academic year and a new IEP plan is made. Some children stay in a resource class for a year, some stay in for four, six or eight years. Some children stay in a resource class for their entire school career.

QUESTION: It seems that if you don't call an IEP meeting, your child will never get the special help they might need?

ANSWER: That's correct.

QUESTION: Why don't the schools talk to parents about IEP meetings?

ANSWER: I don't know. Any parents, after having come to our office, are very appreciative that they found out about IEP's because their children can get the help they need.

The other thing I want to mention is that schools will identify children who need help without a parent initiating it and suggest to the parents that their child be placed in a resource class. It's just that many ADHD children fall through the cracks.

QUESTION: What is that?

ANSWER: There are very specific state guidelines as to who qualifies for the resource classes. Many ADHD children do not meet the state criteria for qualifying and, therefore, are excluded. The schools acknowledge that these children have problems in class as well as problems in learning. However, they say "their hands are tied" because these children do not meet the state guidelines.

QUESTION: What can be done about that if my child fits into this category?

ANSWER: That is one of the main reasons that we do extensive testing at our Center. With a parent's written permission, in the form of a release, we will send the test results to a child's school. Often this can facilitate a child getting the special help he needs.

QUESTION: If my child goes into a resource class, won't everyone know he's a "dummy" and then he'll get teased and labeled by the other children?

ANSWER: There are an awful lot of children who go into resource classes. Approximately 15% to 18% of all students have problems with learning. Your child won't be the only one in the class. It's a relatively common occurrence. The resource teachers are aware of any problems that might exist with the other children and they can help your child deal with situations if they happpen. Again, because resource classes are so common these days, teasing doesn't seem to happen very often.

In any event, the alternative is much worse if your child stayed in a regular class and didn't learn. His self-esteem would be devastated. If your child attends a resource class, he will learn more than in a regular class and he will feel better about himself. Many children will do well in resource classes for a year or two and then they won't need them anymore.

CHAPTER THIRTEEN: Medications

The single major reason mothers don't bring their children to the Center when they suspect they have a problem with ADHD is they're afraid we will put their child on medication.

Over and over mothers have said to me during their initial visit, "I know I should have been here three years ago. I know I should have been here sooner but I don't want my child on medication."

NOTE: THE AUTHOR OF THIS INFORMATION GUIDE, PETER H. BUNTMAN, M.S.W., LCSW IS LICENSED BY THE STATE OF CALIFORNIA, LICENSE NUMBER LCS 4641, AS A LICENSED CLINICAL SOCIAL WORKER. HE IS A STATE LICENSED PSYCHOTHERAPIST WHO SPECIALIZES IN CHILDREN, PRETEEN AND TEENS. HE ALSO SPECIALIZES IN ADHD-RELATED PROBLEMS. HE IS NOT A MEDICAL DOCTOR.

The information that follows in this chapter is about medication. It is the result of information gathered from medical doctors who have specialized in ADHD for the last fifteen years. This is a consensus of their opinions regarding medications and ADHD.

When moms come into our office saying, "I don't want my child on medication," that's actually putting the "cart before the horse." The first task we have is to evaluate the child. We do that by speaking to the mom at length and doing neuropsychological testing. Once we have the results of the evaluation, we sit down with the mother and talk about her choices and options.

Some of the problems that moms come into our office for thinking their child is ADHD won't be helped at all by medication. These include most Learning Disabilities, Oppositional Defiant Disorders and most cases of Childhood Trauma.

There are other problems such as ADHD that could be helped by medication.

Our job in doing the evaluation is to pinpoint exactly what the child has and then speak to the mother about the choices. If, in fact, the testing indicates the child has a problem that could benefit from medication, we will note that in the evaluation and in our discussion with the mother. Then if the mother is interested in medication, we will encourage her to go to her pediatrician, family doctor, or general practitioner to get a prescription.

Some mothers have come to the Center whose religious beliefs don't allow their children to be put on medication. In particular, we've seen a number of families who are Christian Scientists.

The Christian Science religion doesn't believe in medication. We've been able to successfully treat some very difficult cases of ADHD without medication, either when the parents' religious belief forbid it or when the parents just didn't want it.

We know that medication for ADHD children can be effective immediately and help children an awful lot.

When a child is ADHD, our recommendations often include a trial dose to see how the child responds to the medication.

Again, the major stumbling block seems to be the resistance of moms to put their small children on medications.

One reasoning we use to help moms look at the situation is to explain that if their child had juvenile diabetes and a medical doctor recommended insulin, they would give it to him. Or if their child had a severe hearing problem and a doctor recommended a hearing aid, they would get it. Or if their children had a bad case of nearsightedness, they would certainly get him glasses.

ADHD is a genetic problem which is a neuroloical problem that often responds to medication very quickly.

When parents go to a medical doctor, usually one of three "front line drugs" is prescribed. They are Ritalin, Dexedrine and Cylert. All of these drugs are Amphetamines or "uppers." Parents always ask, "If my child has poor impulse control and excess motor activity, wouldn't an "upper" or Amphetamine make him even more hyper?"

Logically it would seem so. But the experience is that these three medications have the opposite effect of slowing the child down, decreasing his motor activity that helps him concentrate and helps with his impulsivity.

No one knows why Amphetamines work with ADHD children. But they do work. Most parents see the results in their children within two hours of giving them the medication.

One of the major reasons parents stop the medication is that there are often side effects. The side effects can include headaches, stomachaches, insomnia, nausea and lack of appetite.

If your child has side effects, and more than 70% of children who take medication seem to have side effects, you need to immediately call your doctor and he will either change the medication, change the dosage or help you with the side effects.

Since each child is different, one of the other issues with medication is that it is often a "trial and error" process of getting the dosage right. Doctors always start out with a very small dose. If that doesn't achieve desired results, they will frequently raise the dosage.

There are also different ways of giving the medication. Some children take their medication once a day, some twice a day, some take time-release where they take it once a day and it's released into the body throughout the day.

Parents who give their children medication need to work very closely with their physician to make sure they are getting the correct dosage and the right format. Whether it's once or twice a day, or time-release and whether it's the right drug to minimize side effects.

Again, it's a "trial and error" process. Until the medication is adjusted you may not get all of the results you want so you will need to keep talking to and going back to your doctor until the medication is adjusted satisfactorily and your child is responding well.

If for any reason these medications are not effective or if your child has serious side effects, often doctors will often go to drugs outside of the Amphetamine or Stimulant family.

Probably the most common one is Imipramine. Tofranil is the product name. Imipramine is an Antidepressant. However, it often is effective on ADHD symptoms and helps with the behavior.

Disadvantages of Imipramine are that it often takes a number of weeks to show an effect on a child. It also needs to be monitored with blood tests and electrocardiograms on a regular basis. This is because the drug can become toxic in the blood stream at high levels.

One of the other commonly prescribed drugs is Clonidine which is an antihypertensive medication. Clonidine can often help with ADHD symptoms.

Again, if your physician recommends Imipramine or a similar drug such as Desipramine, it's crucial and critical to be aware of possible side effects and that they can be toxic at too high levels. It's also crucial and critical that your child be monitored with blood tests and electrocardiograms on a regular basis.

QUESTION: What about medication during the school vacations and summers? Do ADHD children need to be on medication during those times?

AGAIN, I WANT TO EMPHASIZE THAT I'M NOT A MEDICAL DOCTOR. I'M A LICENSED CLINICAL SOCIAL WORKER AND MY EXPERTISE IS IN PSYCHOTHERAPY WITH ADHD CHILDREN, PRETEENS AND TEENS, NOT MEDICATION. THE ANSWERS AND INFORMATION IN THIS CHAPTER ARE A RESULT OF CONVERSATIONS WITH THE MEDICAL DOCTORS AND CHILD PSYCHIATRISTS WE'VE WORKED WITH THROUGHOUT THE YEARS. THEY ARE THOSE DOCTORS' OPINIONS ABOUT MEDICATION AND ADHD.

ANSWER: Very often doctors will suggest continuing medication during school holidays.

The key thing is to report to your physician how your child behaves. If the child's chief problem is while he's at school and school isn't an issue during vacations and summer, then that would be fine. If your child is having all sorts of other problems with impulse control and playing with other children, then you may need to report that to your physican so medication can be used throughout the year so your child can be happy and well adjusted.

If your child's condition is helped by medication, you might want to consider that it might make sense to keep him on medication for the entire year. This issue needs to be discussed thoroughly with your physician.

QUESTION: I had my child on medication for three years. He does better, but we still have a lot of problems with him. What should we do?

ANSWER: Our position is always very clear that medication isn't the only answer. We believe you need medication and short-term family counseling.

The two combined are the best single way to help a child.

CHAPTER FOURTEEN: Questions From Parents

Mr. Buntman frequently lectures to parents about ADHD. His lectures help parents to understand their ADHD child and teaches them how to get their ADHD child under control at school and at home.

The following are some of the most frequently asked questions by parents who attend Mr. Buntman's Lectures on ADHD:

QUESTION FROM PARENT: You talk about "ADHD." What exactly is ADHD? Can a child have Attention Deficit Disorder and not Hyperactivity? Can a child have Hyperactivity and not Attention Deficit Disorder or does he have to have both?

ANSWER: ADHD means Attention Deficit/Hyperactivity Disorder. Attention Deficit is difficulty in the ability to concentrate. The children who have this have problems of inattention. Hyperactivity is a problem of poor impulse control and excessive motor activity or hyperactivity.

With ADHD there are three sub-types or three different categories. The first is when six or more symptoms of attention problems and six or more problems of hyperactivity-impulse control exists and has persisted for at least six months. This is called Attention Deficit Disorder/Hyperactivity Disorder combined type.

The second category is Attention Deficit/Hyperactivity Disorder predominately inattention. This is diagnosed if six or more symptoms of attention problems but fewer of six symptoms of hyperactivity-impulsivity have existed for six months.

The third category is Attention Deficit Disorder/Hyperactivity Disorder predominately hyperactive impulse type. This type is when six or more symptoms of hyperactivity-impulsivity have existed for more than six months but with fewer than six symptoms of inattention.

For the list of the signs and symptoms of ADHD, see pages 8 and 9 of this information guide.

QUESTION FROM PARENT: You say that ADHD is inherited, but what if it doesn't exist in either my husband's or my families?

ANSWER: You need to ask a lot of questions about not only you and your husband and how the two of you were as children but you need to ask your parents and your husband's parents about brothers and sisters and cousins on both sides.

You also need to look at your brothers' and sisters' children to see if they have any of the signs and symptoms of ADHD.

When we meet with parents at our office, we do a lot of questioning. For example; we ask, "How did you do in school?" "How did your brothers or sisters do in school?" "How were their grades?" "Did they ever get into trouble with the teachers?" We ask the same of cousins, aunts and uncles and current cousins of their own children.

We find that parents may not say that their child has ADHD but they may say things that lead to the possibility of it. Parents may tell us things such as, "My dad said my brother always got in trouble at school."

Often a parent will say, "My mom said my brother had a hard time in school. He always got into trouble with his teachers."

If for example, you are 35 and your brother is 45. It stands to reason that when your brother was in school 35 years ago the words "ADHD" may not have been used. However, if you ask your parents and family members if your brother exhibited any of these signs and symptoms, they may confirm he has ADHD behaviors. This is probably the best way to trace ADHD in your family tree.

QUESTION FROM PARENT: Can a child be both ADHD and ODD (Oppositional Defiant Disorder)?

ANSWER: Absolutely.

QUESTION FROM PARENT: How do you tell?

ANSWER: Because the two Disorders have symptoms that are identical, the best way to get a correct diagnosis is to bring your child into a Center that specializes in ADHD and related problems. At our Center, we do an extensive history which simply means we ask the parents a lot of questions and ask them to fill out a long questionnaire. We then do testing with the child to determine an exact diagnosis and then we present the test results to the parent along with a plan of how we can best help their child.

QUESTION FROM PARENT: Can a child have both ADHD and Learning Disabilities?

ANSWER: Absolutely. Again, the best way to determine this is to take your child into a Center that specializes in ADHD-related problems.

As I said before, at our Center we take an extensive case history which means we ask the parents a lot of questions and ask them to complete a long questionnaire. We then do testing with the child to find out exactly what he has.

After the testing is finished, we meet with the parents and present a report of the testing results and suggest ways to best help their child.

Many ADHD children have extreme difficulty learning and doing well in school because of the nature of their problem. After we determine a child is ADHD, we can help the child learn better in school.

We can help a child if learning difficulties in school are just a result of ADHD.

If the testing shows additional learning disabilities, we can also work on that while helping deal with the ADHD.

QUESTION FROM PARENT: When you talk about all of the different problems a child could have, doesn't that make the diagnosis very difficult?

ANSWER: Yes. In addition to all of the other Disorders that a child could have such as ADHD, Oppositional Defiant Disorders or Early Childhood Trauma resulting in anxiety or depression. A child could also have Learning Disabilities, Seizure Disorders, Epilepsy, Lead Poisoning and/or Organicity. There are actually other problems as well. These all could result in symptoms that are similar, if not identical, to ADHD.

QUESTION FROM PARENT: What are some of those?

ANSWER: There's an awful lot of them. Some of the most common ones are:

1. Anoxia, which is a result of loss of oxygen during the birthing process. These children could also have problems with attention and concentration, as well as irritability and poor impulse control. But, again, it has a different basis than ADHD which has a genetic basis.

2. Fetal Alcohol Syndrome, which creates problems that are very similar to ADHD but the basis is different.

3. Any medical reason, such as the loss of consciousness for several days could cause problems of Inattention, Concentrating and Poor Impulse Control.

QUESTION FROM PARENT: You say that at your Center the testing is administered by Neuropsychologists. What is a Neuropsychologist?

ANSWER: Neuropsychologists are Psychologists who have had additional training and specialization in ADHD children and related type problems. This training is usually after their doctorate degree and is post-doctorate training.

QUESTION FROM PARENT: Do you know of any famous people who have ADHD that could be used as examples to children so that children can believe that even with a problem like ADHD people can still be very successful?

ANSWER: It really helps a child to understand that they're not alone and that even some famous people had ADHD. Now of course, since we didn't have the term "ADHD" when these people were around, we can only infer they are ADHD that by their behavior. But it sure seems probable.

One person was Thomas Edison. He was kicked out of his class. In addition to ADHD, he could have had a Learning Disability as well.

Another famous person is Winston Churchill who, from his behavior it seems, could easily have been classified as ADHD.

QUESTION FROM PARENT: Once you find that your child has ADHD, how do you explain it to him?

ANSWER: You want to be sure to use language that is appropriate to the child's age and give examples within their understanding that makes the child feel comfortable.

One way is to talk to the child about how his body works and that children who have ADHD have a hard time stopping themselves.

When we tell children this, most of the time they say, "Yeah, I know. When I tell my body to do something it just doesn't listen! Like it's got a mind of its own."

An older child might say, "My body isn't cooperating with me."

Then you would tell the child, "Were going to do things that will help you to get your body to listen to you, to stop itself and to cooperate with you."

Another way we talk to children and explain ADHD to them is to tell them the motor in their brain goes too fast and that we need to slow it down so that it works together with their body.

Another thing to stress to the child is that there is nothing wrong with him, he's not a "bad" person and that we can help him change whatever is going on in his body. In this way he will be able to control his behavior and feel better about himself, both at school and at home.

ADHD children almost always have a very poor self-image because they're constantly in trouble at home and at school.

QUESTION FROM PARENT: When a child comes to you for counseling, what do you do with the child?

ANSWER: In almost all cases we don't work just with the child but with the entire family unit; the mom, the dad, and the child.

The traditional way of doing therapy with children, teens and adults is what's called "insight" therapy.

Insight therapy works by giving people understanding as to their behaviors. And then as a result, understanding and helping them to change. For example, if an alcoholic, adult man comes into counseling and doesn't understand that he is an alcoholic, the first thing you have to do is "give him insight" to get him to understand he has a problem. This is done by explaining his behavior to him and trying to help him understand it. For example; you tell him that his wife says that he drinks every night and passes out. When his wife goes to work two evenings a week he can't hear his 2- and 3-year-old children cry during the night if he's out cold because he's consumed so much alcohol.

He needs to be told that he drinks at lunch and is very irritable in the afternoons and has alcohol on his breath. By giving him "insight" you've helped him undersatnd.

Insight therapy is totally useless with ADHD children. We do short-term, family therapy. Essentially, this therapy becomes coaching by giving parents specific and detailed directions on what to do with their child when he misbehaves.

Each child is very different. When we have a child and his parents in our counseling office, we see what the child does that's inappropriate. Then we design specific, detailed instructions for the parents to follow that will work best with that specific child.

QUESTION FROM PARENT: I took my child to a psychologist through a counseling program at my work. The psychologist first saw my child alone. Then he saw us alone.

ANSWER: That's the antiquated, old-fashioned way which we don't agree with.

Our short-term counseling emphasizes that the parents must be in the room with the child so that the therapist can see what the child does that's inappropriate. He then gives the parents specific instructions in "coaching" to help get the child to behave.

QUESTION FROM PARENT: What's a "Conduct Disorder?" Is it a form of ADHD or is it like ADHD?

ANSWER: Conduct Disorder is when the behavior of the child repeatedly violates the rights of other people and/or violates rules of society. The characteristics of a Conduct Disorder is that this behavior is repeated.

The following are examples of behavior that are used as the diagnostic criteria for Conduct Disorder. They are taken from pages 90 and 91 of the "Diagnostic and Statistical Manual of Mental Disorders, Fourth Edition" (DSM-IV)

A.   A repetititve and persistent pattern of behavior in which the basic rights of others or major age-approrpiate societal norms or rules are violated, as manifested by the presence of three (or more) of the following criteria in the past 12 months, with at least one criterion present in the past 6 months:

AGGRESSION TO PEOPLE AND ANIMALS

(1)   often bullies, threatens, or intimidates others
(2)   often initiates physical fights
(3)   has used a weapon that can cause serious physical harm to others (e.g., a bat, brick, broken bottle, knife, gun)
(4)   has been physically cruel to people
(5)   has been physically cruel to animals
(6)   has stolen while confronting a victim (e.g., mugging, purse snatching, extortion, armed robbery)
(7)   has forced someone into sexual activity

DESTRUCTION OF PROPERTY

(8)   has deliberately engaged in fire setting with the intention of causing serious damage

(9)   has deliberately destroyed others' property (other than by fire setting)

(10)   has broken into someone else's house, building, or car

(11)   often lies to obtain goods or favors or to avoid obligations (i.e., "cons" others)

(12)   has stolen items of nontrivial value without confronting a victim (e.g., shoplifting, but without breaking and entering; forgery)

SERIOUS VIOLATIONS OF RULES

(13)   often stays out at night despite parental prohibitions, beginning before age 13 years

(14)   has run away from home overnight at least twice while living in parental or parental surrogate home (or once without returning for a lengthy period)

(15)   is often truant from school, beginning before age 13 years

B.   The disturbance in behavior causes clinically significant impairment in social, academic, or occupational functioning.

C.   If the individual is age 18 years or older, criteria are not met for Antisocial Personality Disorder.

Specify type based on age at onset:

CHILDHOOD-ONSET TYPE: Onset of at least one criterion characteristic of Conduct Disorder prior to age 10 years

ADOLESCENT-ONSET TYPE: Absence of any criteria characteristic of Conduct Disorder prior to age 10 years

Specify severity:

MILD: Few, if any, conduct problems in excess of those required to make the diagnosis and conduct problems cause only minor harm to others

MODERATE: Number of conduct problems cause only minor harm to others between "mild" and "severe"

SEVERE: Many conduct problems in excess of those required to make the diagnosis or conduct problems cause considerable harm to others

QUESTION FROM PARENT: Can a child be ADHD and have a Conduct Disorder?

ANSWER: Yes.

QUESTION FROM PARENT: Can a child be Conduct Disorder and Oppositionally Defiant Disorder at the same time?

ANSWER: No. If symptoms from both are present, we address it as "Conduct Disorder" and we don't say "Oppositional Defiant Disorder."

QUESTION FROM PARENT: Do you have any opinion about biofeedback for ADHD children?

ANSWER: The research is clear that there's no definitive study that says biofeedback is effective for ADHD children.

In the last five or six years, about 20 parents have come to the Center and told me they've taken their children for biofeedback. Of the 20, about 7 (which is about 1/3) have said it's helped with their children's behavior. Of all the parents that we've spoken with, they've said it helped most when they went to counseling as well.

FOR ADDITIONAL COPIES OF LIVING WITH YOUR ADHD CHILDREN

dditional copies of *Living With Your ADHD Children* are available for $11.95, plus $3.00 shipping and handling (all books are shipped priority mail).

me_____

ddress_____

y_____ State_____ Zip_____

ving With Your ADHD Children:

____ copies @ $11.95 =	_____	
7.75% Sales Tax (CA res. only)	_____	NAME:_____
Shipping/Handling		
($3.00 first copy,		ADDRESS: _____
$2.00 each add'l copy)	_____	
TOTAL	_____	CITY_____ STATE_____ ZIP CODE_____

I have enclosed a check in the amount above.
Please bill my ☐ MasterCard, ☐ Visa, ☐ Discover or ☐ American Express.
edit Card Number:_____Exp. Date_____   SIGNATURE: _____

il *your order to:*

CENTER FOR FAMILY LIFE, INC.
3611 Farquhar Avenue, Suite 3
Los Alamitos, CA 90720

x orders 24 hours a day to: (562) 596-4601

We Offer a 100% Money-Back Guarantee

If for any reason, within one year after you receive your order, you are not 100% satisfied, you may return the items, and you will get a 100% refund --
no questions asked.

---

re's more *MUST* resources for parents with ADHD children:

lp For Parents With Hyperactive Kids, by Dr. Paul Wittenberg, Licensed Psychologist, $9.95 audio cassette tape. In this information packed tape, Dr. Wittenberg teaches parents step-by-p directions on specifically and exactly what to do when Hyperactive/ADD kids don't listen and have problems at home. You can immediately apply Dr. Wittenberg's step-by-step specific thodology when you are finished listening to the tape. Normal punishments frequently don't work for Hyperactive/ADD children, but Dr. Wittenberg's proven techniques and directions will p your child to behave at home and at school. Dr. Wittenberg is a nationally known Psychologist who specializes in working with Hyperactive/ADD kids. This is a must to be listened to orded session because on the tape Dr. Wittenberg teaches parents of Hyperactive/ADD kids different ways to regain control and how to live with the ADHD children.

elp For Moms With Hyperactive Kids" gives more practical and succinct information to parents than any other tape I've used in my 27 years or practice. Not only is this tape helpful for ents, it is equally helpful to psychologists, teachers and the MFCC working with children and families. This tape gives the parent and the professional a very well organized format from ich to work/parent from." *Dr. Robert Dienstag, Neuropsychologist, ADHD Specialist*

w *To Live Harmoniously With Your Children & Teens,* Four Tape Audio Cassette Series In An Album: $37.50. *How To Nurture Self-Esteem In A Child And Teen,* by Peter H. ntman, M.S.W., ACSW, LCSW. Everyone talks about "self-esteem" being necessary for children and teens. In this tape, Mr. Buntman teaches parents how to nurture self-esteem for ldren and teens alike. *Attentive Listening*, by Peter H. Buntman, M.S.W., ACSW, LCSW. In this tape, Mr. Buntman teaches the most difficult skill of attentive parental listening, how to rn these skills and how to communicate with your child. *Straight Talk* by Peter H. Buntman, M.S.W., ACSW, LCSW. Parents have a difficult time dealing with their anger towards your ld. On this tape, Mr. Buntman teaches the techniques of straight talk, how to deal with your anger in a constructive way, and how to get your child and teens to listen, understand, hear you, d obey you. *Anger And Child and Teen Problems* by Peter H. Buntman, M.S.W., ACSW, LCSW. On this tape, Mr. Buntman teaches constructive versus destructive ways to handle ental constructive ways to handle anger, both from the perspective of an angry parent and an angry child/or adolescent. *ALL 4 AUDIO CASSETTE TAPES ABOVE IN AN ALBUM 7.50.*

he listeners of this very well organized tape series will not waste one minute of time. Each tape is crammed with very worthwhile information that parents will find useful on a daily basis. e information explains step-by-step how to correct and prevent conflicts between parents and their children and teens. This is an invaluable parenting tool for parents with children and teens. e tape series is especially valuable for parents of ADHD children because it helps moms deal with their anger towards their children and tells moms how to build their child's self-esteem.
        Dr. Robert Dienstag, Neuropsychologist, ADHD Specialist

____ copies @ $11.95 *"Living With Your ADHD Children"*	_____
____ copies @ $ 9.95 *"Help For Parents With Hyperactive Kids"*	_____
____ copies @ $37.50 *"How To Live Harmoniously With Your Children & Teens,"*	_____
(A Four Tape Audio Cassette Series In An Album)	
7.75% Sales Tax (CA res. only)	_____
Shipping/Handling (All Books Shipped Priority Mail)	
($3.00 first item	
$2.00 each additional copy)	_____
TOTAL	_____

I have enclosed a check in the amount above.   NAME: _____

Please bill my ☐ MasterCard, ☐ Visa, ☐ Discover or ☐ American Express.   ADDRESS: _____
edit Card Number: _____ Exp. Date_____
                                                 CITY_____STATE_____ ZIP CODE_____
il *your order to:*   **CENTER FOR FAMILY LIFE, INC.**
                3611 Farquhar Avenue, Suite 3
                Los Alamitos, CA 90720   SIGNATURE: _____

x orders 24 hours a day at: (800) 550-6656   --i--